Becoming an Occupational Therapist

Is occupational therapy really the career for you?

Second edition

Chris McKenna and Cath Wright

BPP
UNIVERSITY
SCHOOL OF HEALTH

First edition 2012
Second edition 2016

ISBN 9781 5097 0236 7
Previous ISBN 9781 4453 9730 6
e-ISBN 9781 5097 0270 1
e-ISBN 9781 5097 0269 5

British Library Cataloguing-in-Publication Data
A catalogue record for this book is available from the British Library

Published by
BPP Learning Media Ltd
BPP House, Aldine Place
London W12 8AA

www.bpp.com/health

Printed in the United Kingdom by
RICOH UK Limited
Unit 2
Wells Place
Merstham
RH1 3LG

Your learning materials, published by BPP Learning Media Ltd, are printed on paper sourced from sustainable, managed forests.

The views expressed in this book are those of BPP Learning Media and not those of UCAS or any universities. BPP Learning Media are in no way associated with or endorsed by UCAS or any universities.

The contents of this book are intended as a guide and not professional advice. Although every effort has been made to ensure that the contents of this book are correct at the time of going to press, BPP Learning Media, makes no warranty that the information in this book is accurate or complete and accept no liability for any loss or damage suffered by any person acting or refraining from acting as a result of the material in this book.

Every effort has been made to contact the copyright holders of any material reproduced within this publication. If any have been inadvertently overlooked, BPP Learning Media will be pleased to make the appropriate credits in any subsequent reprints or editions.

Contents

Free companion material

Readers can access additional companion material for free online.

To access companion material please visit **www.bpp.com/freehealthresources**.

About the publisher

The UK's only university solely dedicated to business and the professions.

We are dedicated to preparing you for a professional career. We offer a strong commercial approach, within a business culture designed to help you stand out in the workplace after you graduate. Our programmes are designed in partnership with employers and respected professionals in the fields of law, business, finance and health.

About the authors

Chris McKenna is the programme leader for the MSc Occupational Therapy (pre-registration) in the School of Health & Social Care at Teesside University and has interviewed potential occupational therapy students for over 10 years. Chris helps occupational therapists understand and use occupational therapy theory. Current areas of interest are the work ethic and individual motivation, and sensory profiling in schools.

Cath Wright is a senior lecturer and admissions tutor for Occupational Therapy at Teesside University. Cath has had experience in a wide variety of practice areas and had responsibility for a range of inter-professional teams. Her interests lie within leadership and service development and her current research is in the area of co-dependence.

Foreword

If you are keen to know more about occupational therapy, and to decide whether it is the right career for you, read on.

In common with other professions, occupational therapy cannot be described in one sentence; it is a broad and complex profession that provides challenge and intrinsic reward, hopefully in equal measure!

This publication will help you to gain a better understanding of what being an occupational therapist is all about. It will help you to consider which training route to pursue, explain what the training involves and provide some helpful tips and guidance to ensure you succeed in your career journey.

In common with other professions, and as much as we try to avoid it, the world of occupational therapy does have technical jargon that can be hard to understand. This book will help you to demystify the jargon, to understand more about the profession and the education to prepare you for it, and to succeed in your endeavours to become an occupational therapist. In addition, it helpfully signposts where you might go to find further information.

Enjoy the book and if you decide to proceed, enjoy your student journey. We at the British Association and College look forward to welcoming you into the professional community.

Julia Scott
Chief Executive,
British Association and
College of Occupational Therapists

Acknowledgements

We would like to thank all of our colleagues, students and occupational therapists who have contributed case studies and personal insights for this book so generously. We would also like to thank Claire Brewis and Linda McCann for their advice and expertise.

Chris would also like to acknowledge the love and support of Rachel, Isaac, Jemima, Abel and Isabella who have enabled this to happen and the generations of occupational therapists from whom we all learn.

Cath is grateful to Mark, Amy and Adam for their encouragement and to Peter Woodall who was the inspiration for her career choice.

Shining a light on your future career path

The process of researching and identifying a career that you are most suited to can be a somewhat daunting process, but the rewards of following a career that truly engages you should not be underestimated. Deciding on your future career path should be viewed as a fun and extremely satisfying process that, if done correctly, will benefit you greatly.

Carefully considering a short list of future career options and what each one will offer you will help you to make a truly informed decision. Although it is perfectly acceptable to change career direction at a later date, reviewing the options open to you now will help to ensure that you are satisfied with your career from the outset.

I first began mentoring aspiring professionals ten years ago when it was clear that many individuals were not gaining access to the careers guidance they required. It was with this in mind that I embarked on publishing our *Becoming a* series of books, to provide help, support and clear insight into career choices. I hope that this book will help you to make an informed decision as to what career you are most suited to, your strengths and your aspirations.

I would like to take this opportunity to wish you the very best of luck with identifying your future career and hope that you pass on some of the gems of wisdom that you acquire along the way, to those who follow in your footsteps.

Matt Green
Series Editor – *Becoming a* series
Director of Professional Development
BPP University

Chapter 1

Introduction and overview

BPP
UNIVERSITY
SCHOOL OF HEALTH

As with the first edition this book provides information to help you make an informed decision about your future as an occupational therapist. Choosing a career is a difficult process and this book will help to make that decision easier. You may be considering attending university for the first time or perhaps returning to university. This will bring about great change for you whatever your situation. Decisions about leaving home, changing career and choosing the right course are all very important at this time and this book will discuss the options available to you.

While much of the content relates to the general university experience in the United Kingdom the main focus throughout is the study of occupational therapy itself. Many of the frequently asked questions about occupational therapy education are answered and where this has not been possible you will be directed to the best place to locate this information. This book provides answers to the sorts of questions you need to consider before deciding if occupational therapy is for you.

There are a number of areas which potential students find confusing. In Chapter 3 consideration is given to the level of study and the manner of delivery of the course material. You will be given information about the kinds of assessment you might expect to undertake as well as information to help you choose a university appropriate to your personal circumstances. The application process is considered in Chapter 4 including what the admissions team will be looking for in your personal statement and at interview. Your expectations of life as a student may have been generated by the anecdotes of others and reports in the media. Here you will find an objective viewpoint. Chapter 5 includes information about finance, equipment, the potential facilities and support offered at the university. As finance is one of the major considerations for any new student this area of potential stress is explored in Chapter 6.

The mystery of what you will actually study has been broken down in Chapter 7 and Chapter 9. The content of curricula has been uncovered to give you an insight into the main areas of study and how the early learning provides an underpinning for later study. These chapters are separated by Chapter 8 which considers the practice placement element of the course. This is often the element of the programme which students most enjoy. The variety of placements available is discussed including the new concept of role emerging placements.

Occupational therapy helps people to engage as independently as possible in the things they want to do in order to enhance their health and wellbeing. Those who pursue a career in occupational therapy should already understand the importance of the profession in effecting change in the lives of service users and their carers. In Chapter 11 and Chapter 12 the different opportunities for occupational therapists to practise in once they have graduated are investigated. It is not possible to cover every area of practice due to the extensive range of existing roles and the continuous development of new practice areas. Some consideration has been given to potential practice roles and a series of case studies have been included to illustrate some of the existing roles of the occupational therapist. Chapter 13 reminds us that occupational therapists are part of an international profession with international links and responsibilities. It introduces you to the World Federation of Occupational Therapists, the Council of Occupational Therapists for the European Countries and the international agenda at this time.

Chapter 14 closes the book with a series of narratives. Each explores a real day in the life of an occupational therapist. These stories help you appreciate the reality of practice and to provide a flavour of the opportunities which await a practitioner.

You are at the threshold of a new and exciting career.

Case study: Why I chose to do occupational therapy – Mary Mulholland

'I chose occupational therapy because I want to be what I believe I am "best fitted to become" (Wilcock, 1998). I believe that occupational therapy best fits my nature, personality and life philosophy. People and their motivations have always fascinated me. From being a young girl I have always enjoyed sharing a close connection with people. Listening, observing and seeking understanding of what makes sense to them, what makes them tick? In my younger years, I was unaware that these fascinations were career transferable and started my employment within the capitalist machine. This did not fit with my core values and beliefs. I have gained an understanding and an eagerness to learn more about the effects of what we do, or in turn, what we are unable to do has on a person's sense of self, health and wellbeing. When I discovered occupational therapy I saw an opportunity to be part of a profession that shared my fascinations, values and core beliefs; a community that values a deep understanding of people, their needs and motivations. A professional ethos that promotes holistic care through facilitating positive change with a proactive person centred approach.

Finally, I chose occupational therapy because I truly believe in its unique philosophy.'

People will commence their training for their own reasons and this book will serve you well as a resource throughout your training and beyond. It will give focus and direction to your personal research and should enable you to confidently select an appropriate programme, submit a more relevant application and prepare for an interview. This book has been designed to help you succeed in the career of your choice. The questions it answers and the ideas raised will help facilitate that success. The rest is up to you.

Chapter summary

Occupational therapy may be your first choice of career. That decision will have been guided by your own, very personal circumstances. Others will have made a similar decision in the past and have pursued very fulfilling careers. As you embark on a journey to become an occupational therapist you will develop skills and gain great knowledge of the profession until you can walk across the stage at graduation to applause from friends and family; from there you will enter your first post in what will be a rewarding and successful career.

Key points

- You should do plenty of research before deciding on a career in occupational therapy.
- Think about what you want to get out of your career.
- Think about what you want to study, where you want to study and how you want to study.
- Make sure you gain a good understanding of the profession in a range of different settings.
- Reflect on why you want to be an occupational therapist.

Useful resources

The College of Occupational Therapists: www.cot.co.uk

NHS Careers: www.nhscareers.nhs.uk/

Chapter 2

How do I know that occupational therapy is the right career for me?

BPP UNIVERSITY SCHOOL OF HEALTH

Definition

Occupational therapy is the assessment and treatment of physical and psychiatric conditions (NHS, 2012).

Occupational therapists use specific, purposeful activities to maintain healthy lifestyles, to prevent disability and promote independent function in all aspects of daily life. Occupational therapists work in a huge variety of settings. This might include hospitals, schools, prisons, social care, industry, and voluntary and charitable organisations. Occupational therapists also visit clients and their carers at home.

Occupational therapists work with babies, young children, adolescents, adults and older people to help them overcome the effects of disability caused by physical or psychological illness, ageing or accident. The profession offers enormous opportunities for career development and endless variety.

What do you want from your career?

By now you will have considered the factors that you feel will be important in your future career. Are you looking for opportunities to help people make positive changes, to enable people to live, work and play as independently and successfully as possible? Are you interested in researching and developing new treatments or assistive equipment? Does the thought of teaching and helping others to learn inspire you? Do you wish to be a leader? If so, then occupational therapy will certainly fulfil these needs. If you are looking for a job as a carer; doing things for people and offering sympathy then you are probably not going to find occupational therapy is the job for you.

> *'I enjoy solving problems and thinking creatively. I found working in a rural community, where the majority of houses were old cottages and farms, that I had to use all my imagination to access and adapt my patient's living space. Each day had a different challenge and that made my work varied and enjoyable.'*

Occupational therapists use their unique skills to enable individuals to regain and maintain their maximum level of independence in all their chosen occupations. They work with people of all ages in many different situations. These people may have physical, mental health or social problems resulting from the effects of age, an illness or an accident – or a combination of all three. From the simplest activity to the most complex, occupational therapists analyse the requirements for success and facilitate the process to achieve a realistic goal. They work alongside their patients, ensuring their views are taken into account.

If you were thinking that occupational therapists might not be involved in some of the things nurses do – like taking people to the toilet and other intimate tasks – then this is quite wrong. You may need to be involved in areas of people's lives that are very personal, when a person may be vulnerable. For example, you may be involved in assessing someone wash and dress, you might discuss continence issues or you might need to advise on matters relating to intimacy. You should be prepared to face any topic your client feels is important to them and be able to to work in some testing situations.

Can someone with a disability be an occupational therapist?

The Health and Care Professions Council (HCPC) is a regulatory body set up to maintain a register of health and care professionals who meet the required standards for safe and professional practice.

As long as you can meet the health requirements to register with the HCPC there should be no reason why you could not undertake the training to become an occupational therapist. Universities have support in place for people with specific learning needs. There are occupational therapists in practice who are visually impaired or who are deaf; some occupational therapists have dyslexia and some have mental health conditions.

What are the qualities of a good occupational therapist?

Occupational therapists need a range of skills, some of which you may already have and some of which you can learn. The skills can be divided into personal skills, practical skills and academic skills (see Figure 2.1). It is important to develop all of these skills equally – it will not be possible to 'get by' with great academic skills if you find it very difficult to communicate with others or find it hard to carry out practical tasks.

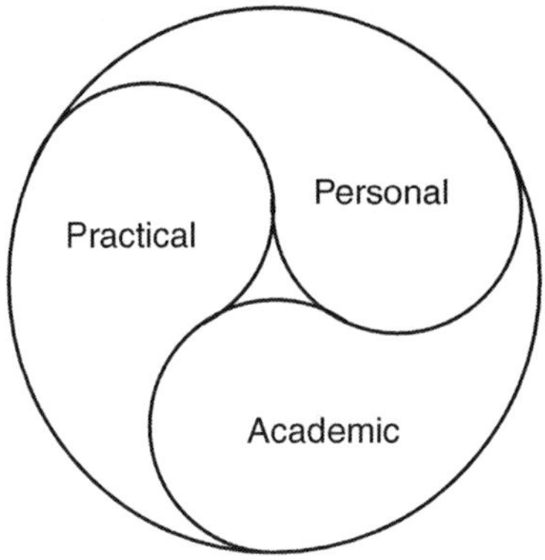

Figure 2.1: The range of occupational therapy skills

Personal skills

You will need to be a patient person, able to sit back and allow someone to tackle an activity at their own pace. If you get frustrated easily or feel you always need to be in control then you might find occupational therapy a frustrating career. Energy, resilience, determination and open mindedness are also essential. You will need excellent communication skills: written, verbal and non-verbal, and you should feel comfortable in the company of people of all ages, sexes, races and cultures. There is no room for discrimination in this career. You will need to demonstrate respectful and dignity focused actions. You will need to be calm, confident and assertive. You will need these personal values and skills and will be able to advance them during your training.

Practical skills

You may already have practical and creative skills which will be useful. For example, you may enjoy painting, pottery, cooking, gardening, sports, drama, sewing or any of a huge range of different activities. An occupational therapist may be involved in making splints or pressure garments for people, in measuring individuals for wheelchairs and rehabilitation equipment, in drawing up plans for housing adaptations or planning treatment sessions involving a range of activities. You can learn new activities and how to use them in a therapeutic way in university and while on placement.

Most practical people consider themselves to be good at problem-solving and this is certainly a skill that occupational therapists have in abundance. A creative, positive mind is essential, as you will need to be able to think of and assess a range of options and alternatives to assist and enable your client. In this profession your only option is to consider all possibilities; to think otherwise limits the potential opportunities.

Academic skills

These include literacy and numeracy skills, as all programmes will require you to have at least a GCSE (or equivalent) pass in both English Language and Mathematics. You may also need to have a science GCSE and should check with the universities which you are interested in to ensure you meet their criteria. Each university will also ask for A Level (or equivalent) qualifications and you will need to check each university for their requirements. All of the information can be found on the university website, in their prospectus or on the College of Occupational Therapists website.

You will also need to be able to think critically about a subject. This means being able to assess information from all angles and feeling confident in drawing conclusions from your thoughts. The academic skills you will learn during your training are research skills, searching for information, referencing, reflecting and analysing.

What relevant experience should I get?

It would be sensible to try to arrange an opportunity to shadow an occupational therapist before you apply to join a training programme. Many students say that they have come across occupational therapy due to either having experienced occupational therapy themselves or having observed the work of an occupational therapist with a relative or friend. This is very useful; however, it will only give a narrow view on this complex profession, so it is advisable to seek out other opportunities to see occupational therapy in action. As well as this, there are some very helpful resources on the College of Occupational Therapists website: video clips with service users, carers and occupational therapists describing the work and its impact on people's lives.

All universities offer a range of discovery days and open days to enable you to decide which programme to choose. Admissions tutors are happy to help you with information and there is usually an opportunity to meet with students who are already undertaking the programme. Lots of the occupational therapy training programmes have Facebook pages or Twitter feeds, where you can communicate with staff and students to get a feel of the programme and profession.

If you find it difficult to get a work placement or shadowing experience then giving some time to volunteer at a care home, for a youth group, as a Scout or Guide leader, at a school, day centre or with a charity will certainly give you an insight into working with a wide variety of people.

Working in a team

There will hardly ever be a situation when an occupational therapist is not working as part of a team. While you are at university there will be plenty of opportunities to develop your team-working skills as you undertake projects and research together. There will be groups and societies to join and many occupational therapy programmes have an occupational therapy society. You can also join the local British Association of Occupational Therapists group and get involved with promoting occupational therapy, learning events and trade union activities. Being part of the professional community as a student member is time well spent, as it helps you to network with professionals and gives you access to a whole range of learning resources via the College of Occupational Therapists.

Assess your skills

Some team skills you will need are shown in Table 2.1. Which of these do you already have and which do you need to develop?

Listening	Negotiation	Reliability	Honesty
Trustworthiness	Communication	Understanding	Patience
Selflessness	Motivation	Assertiveness	Humility
Supportive	Responsive	Approachable	Collaboration

Table 2.1: Team skills for occupational therapy

Teams in practice will include a wide range of other professionals, volunteers, carers, families and of course your service users. Learning to work together and understand each other's roles is very important. This is referred to as 'inter-professional working' and occupational therapists tend to find that they have been well equipped to work like this because of the nature of their profession and due to the training they have received (McKenna and Wright, 2012).

After you have qualified and had some experience working in practice, you might choose to apply for a team leader role. This could be within an occupational therapy team or an inter-professional team.

Top tip

You will need to demonstrate your team-working competency in your UCAS personal statement. There are several ways you could do this, for example, if you have experience working in a team before in either a paid or voluntary capacity, if you have been an active member of a sports team, if you have been a young leader in Scouts or Guides and have earned your scout belt, if you have been part of a church group or if you have undertaken your Duke of Edinburgh's award. Reflect on your experiences and try to show how you have used them to develop your skills.

Understanding and communicating with people

As an occupational therapist you will be communicating with a wide range of people on a day to day basis. Occupational therapists work in a very wide range of services with people of all ages and cultures. You will need to have (or will need to develop) a range of communication styles, so that you feel confident and competent speaking in any given situation. During your training you will be given the opportunity to develop your verbal communication skills, by taking part in presentations, mock interviews, debates, ward rounds and team meetings and you may have the opportunity to attend conflict resolution training. You will work with different students, lecturers and practice staff and learn when to switch from a formal style of communication to informal, as well as developing a style that is business-focused and a style that is person-focused.

During your training you will also develop your written communication skills. It is important that occupational therapists can write up their patient contact notes, write formal letters, and compose reports, service improvement plans and business cases. Writing up contemporaneous notes is a fundamental essential, so you will be given lots of opportunities to develop this skill.

Case study: Developing my skills – Laura Gillett

'Throughout my three years on the BSc (Hons) Occupational Therapy programme I have developed a number of key skills which have benefited me both personally and professionally. Through informative lectures, seminars, assignments and the feedback provided from tutors, I have noticed a vast improvement in my academic skills and feel more confident in regards to carrying out research, reflections and utilising the evidence base to inform my practice. Previously, presenting to a group of individuals was an area of difficulty for me; however, through various assessments carried out over the three years and the support provided from tutors I feel that my presentation skills have largely developed and my confidence has grown. One area that was most influential in developing my skills was my practice placements. I have had the opportunity to work collaboratively with other members of staff, service users and families. This in turn enabled me to improve all aspects of my communication skills such as verbal, non-verbal, electronic and written, whilst also developing my listening skills. Placements have also provided me with opportunities to demonstrate and develop my occupational therapy core skills whilst in practice, this included carrying out assessments, problem-solving and using activity as a therapeutic tool. Finally, the programme has been incredibly beneficial in enabling me to further develop my personal skills of compassion and empathy and enabled me to utilise my skill of creativity for the benefit of service users.'

Two of the skills you will need to develop are active listening and observation. Occupational therapists spend time listening to their clients; after all, the client's views on their condition will help the occupational therapist to formulate the optimum treatment plan. Occupational therapists also watch how their clients undertake practical activities and assess behaviours.

Assess your skills

- Listen to a friend talking about something they have been doing. Afterwards, write down as much as you can remember – all the little details – and then ask your friend to check to see if you remembered correctly.
- Watch how someone makes a hot drink. Can you spot all the different movements they make? Do they make it the same way that you would? Do they follow a sequence?

You will need to assess your own non-verbal communication too. It is important that your actions match your words and that your face does not send a message to a client that might be misunderstood. For example, if you walked into a house that was dirty and had an unpleasant aroma, would you be able to carry on without screwing up your face? It is easy to lose your client's trust if they see you reacting negatively.

What is the occupation in occupational therapy?

The occupation in occupational therapy is activity. It could be any sort of activity, both physical and mental, and is all of the things that an individual needs and wants to do in their everyday life.

Hardly a moment goes by without an activity happening. Even during the night people are actively engaging in sleeping. Occupational therapy is about helping people to be able to do as much as they can for themselves.

Occupational therapists believe that occupation (activity) can have a positive effect on health. These activities are what defines an individual, what they do and what they can become (Wilcock, 2001). Occupations link together to influence the whole person so physical activity can affect mental activity which can affect social activity. When one or more is damaged, either permanently or semi-permanently, the whole person feels the effect. Occupational therapists see everyone as a whole person. So if someone has a broken hip, an occupational therapist would be concerned with how the fracture affected mobility, mood and the ability to socialise.

Now consider all the actions you observed when someone made a hot drink. Would all of these actions have been possible if you had, for example, lost a limb? How about if you had rheumatoid arthritis or if you were experiencing a period of depression? Of course, there are so many different illnesses and disabilities and each one will have different effects on different people. It is the role of the occupational therapist to understand the physiology and psychology of different illnesses and disabilities and then to use this knowledge in the context of the client and their individual situation. It's like putting together a jigsaw, fitting all the important factors into place to enable the client to feel as independent as they can be.

Occupations are not just the big activities; they are all the small component parts that build together. If one of the component parts is damaged then this can result in a range of other activities being affected too. For example, if you broke both wrists you wouldn't be able to bend them – so what sort of activities would you be unable to do and what would be the consequences in the long and short term? As an occupational therapist you will be considering all of these factors with your client and working together to get the best possible outcomes, based on their goals.

Many people describe occupational therapy in different ways and you will find that you will often have to explain to people the nature of your profession. If you are planning to spend some time with occupational therapists you can ask them how they describe their role – you'll gain a different perspective on the role every time!

So, might occupational therapy be the career for you? The information in this chapter will have helped you to reflect on your own skills and given you the chance to see which of these you can transfer into your career. You will have considered the privileged position an occupational therapist is in when working with vulnerable people and contemplated if you would be able to work comfortably in these situations. One thing is for sure, occupational therapy is an exciting and challenging profession. All you need to do now is decide where to undertake your training!

Chapter summary

Many students have a personal reason for wanting to become an occupational therapist. As occupational therapy can be many things to many people, the key to successful study is an open mind and the ability to see things from as many viewpoints as possible. Once you have assessed your personal skills you will have a baseline for the start of your study. You can be sure that, with so many interesting topics to cover, your training programme will fly by and you will be eagerly preparing for your first post.

Chapters 11 and 12 provide a range of examples of the work occupational therapists might be involved in and provide a good starting point for understanding the role of occupational therapists.

Key points

- Try to meet up with or shadow occupational therapists in both physical and mental health roles.
- Occupational therapists need a mixture of academic, personal and practical skills.
- You will need team-working skills and excellent observation and listening skills.
- You will need patience and be able to sit back and allow someone to try to do things for themselves.
- Your non-verbal communication needs to match your verbal communication.

Useful resources

The College of Occupational Therapists: www.cot.co.uk

References

McKenna, C and Wright, C. (2012) Occupational Therapists. In: Littlechild, B and Smith, R ed. (2012) *A Handbook for Inter-professional Practice in the Human Services: Learning to Work Together*. Edinburgh: Pearson. pp. 249–259.

NHS careers (2012) *Occupational Therapist*. [Online] Available at: www.nhscareers.nhs.uk/explore-by-career/allied-health-professions/careers-in-the-allied-health-professions/occupational-therapist/ [Accessed 27 May 2016].

Wilcock, A (2001) *Occupation for Health*. London: The Lavenham Press Limited.

Chapter 3

How do I choose which course and university to apply to?

BPP UNIVERSITY SCHOOL OF HEALTH

Deciding how and where you should study can be a very difficult decision to make and will involve people other than yourself. Take the time to discuss this with others. Parents, guardians, partners, spouses and children all have a significant voice which should be considered in the decision-making process as they are going to be affected. Teachers and admissions tutors will have experience and perspectives which they will be happy to share with you. In all cases they wish you to have the best experience and the best opportunities. There are also many support websites and books which will provide you with information on occupational therapy. Tap into this knowledge and make your judgements based on the best available information. Organisations such as the College of Occupational Therapists have literature and webpages dedicated to the interested student. As you consider individual programmes and universities, explore their prospectuses and their websites to ensure that you are fully informed regarding what they offer.

This chapter provides you with advice on what to look for as you explore the available information. It will also help you to determine what is important to you in the decision-making process. As you review each section try to note what your preference is for each issue as this will help you to focus your thinking. Please note that references to universities in this book will focus purely on the occupational therapy programmes and the information given should not be assumed for any other programmes delivered at that institution.

Location – does it matter?

We are all different. While some have a preference to live close to family and friends, others prefer to live far away. The locations of universities fall into different categories. There are those which are based in a city centre campus; others are out of town. In some, occupational therapy is taught in the same location as the rest of the student body; in others occupational therapy students are taught separately from the rest of the university. This section explores these differences and considers the advantages and limitations of each.

Some universities are based further out of town like Plymouth University or the University of Northampton and offer a range of opportunities. Things are usually quieter both on and off campus and this will suit those who prefer fewer distractions than being in a city centre. Access to facilities may be limited to those provided by the university and to access community facilities it may be that you require a car or will need to make use of local public transport and taxi services in order to fully experience student life.

Many universities, such as London South Bank, Coventry and Teesside Universities, are located close to the city centre. These universities are situated next to the main shopping thoroughfares and are also very close to main train stations and bus stations. For you, as a student, this can be a life saver (or at least a money saver). Being close to the town means that you have access to all the facilities you need without having to travel far. The cost of living will be greatly reduced as taxis or bus fares may not be required and you may be able to walk home from nights out. Being close to social and shopping spaces also helps you to keep busy and means there is always something to do away from the university. There may be some disadvantages however. For example, accommodation may be older and may be adapted rather than purpose built. That being said, universities have done much to counteract these problems and provide excellent accommodation for students.

'I was determined to study in a city as I had lived in a remote village. I wanted to challenge myself and moving to Salford certainly did that. I hoped to see a different side to life and the placements I went on enabled me to consider issues I had never come across before. It helped me grow and I liked it so much I stayed there after I qualified.'

Occasionally, universities have expanded beyond their original campus to use alternative sites. This could mean the occupational therapy programme is delivered off the main campus. It may also mean students are separated from the main student facilities including the library. While this separation may suit some students, making them feel exceptional, it may make others feel isolated from the rest of the student body. This is a rare situation, as most programmes will be delivered on a campus with the rest of the students and accessible onsite facilities, however it is worth considering such a scenario when thinking about where to apply.

Where the course is based should be considered when choosing where to study. If you have already been to university you may be less interested in what is on campus or what social life is available. Certain towns and cities might be more appealing and the actual campus less relevant. These issues should be considered when deciding where to study.

Top tip

When you go to look at the university, have a look at the town or city too. If you can stay overnight you will get a feel for the location at different times of day and this might help you to make your final decision.

Should I live at home?

This may not be a concern for some students. For many the decision regarding where to study is dictated by finance, family commitment and convenience. For those seeking a new life and adventure then this might not even be a topic for discussion. If you are unsure you may wish to consider the following points.

Leaving home can be a difficult decision. It demands that you begin to fend for yourself. You will have all the freedom you have ever wanted. No one will tell you what to do, there are no rules, you can eat what you want and get up when you like. As in all situations in life there are obligations and responsibilities associated with these rights. You have to look after yourself: this means doing your own cooking, your own laundry and your own cleaning up. Occasionally you might even consider doing your own ironing. You also have to take responsibility for your own bills – rent, TV, internet, Council Tax, water, electricity and gas. The accommodation you choose may include some of these elements, but the costs will still need to be met. Being away from home also means you may feel homesick. Many students experience this to some extent and it will lessen over time, but it can be distracting from your studies.

Living at home can also bring its own difficulties. As you are developing your skills as an adult and trying to maintain a degree of independence, this can be challenged by a well-meaning family. As you are trying to learn, the demands of the family may distract you from your studies. This can be particularly difficult when you are working on assignments or trying to meet submission deadlines. It can also be difficult bringing home new university friends. If you are commuting some distance it may be hard for you to mix with the other students on your course who are in halls together or able to socialise together more easily.

Ultimately this decision will be based on who you are, your commitments and what you want from the experience. Only you can decide what you have at home and what the university can offer you.

What courses are available?

The College of Occupational Therapists website contains a complete list of all courses accredited by the College in the United Kingdom. It shows a great number of different programmes across the country. These have been developed, in the main, as variations of the standard undergraduate programme.

The three-year BSc (Honours) route is the standard programme across England and Wales. In Scotland this route is a four-year programme. This route normally runs full time from September and will accommodate the majority of A Level or equivalent applicants but will also accept students who may have already completed a degree previously.

Accelerated postgraduate programmes have become popular over the past few years. These routes run full time over a period of two years. They cater for applicants who have already completed a degree in another subject but wish to train as an occupational therapist. For some of these programmes there is an expectation that applicants hold a degree in a related subject or that they have some experience working in health or social care. On successful completion of the programme graduates are awarded a Postgraduate Diploma in Occupational Therapy or an MSc in Occupational Therapy. Both of these awards will normally be accepted by the Health and Care Professions Council for registration purposes.

The in-service BSc Honours degree or part-time BSc Honours degree are part-time programmes which have been developed for staff currently working in a support role within health or social care. They undertake the four-year programme with the support of their employer. Attendance is normally two days a week and the student continues in their employed role for the remainder of the week.

There are a number of part-time BSc Honours degree programmes which are similar to the in-service routes but it is not necessary for the applicant to be working in health or social care. When considering the part-time route it is important to clarify the entry requirements.

Students can also undertake a full-time work-based learning BSc Honours degree. This takes two and a half years to complete. Students are employed by a sponsoring organisation and are required to work there following the completion of their programme.

In the long term you must apply for whichever programme is best for you. There may be no choice for some people while others may have a number of options. Although you may already work in healthcare it may not be convenient to undertake a part-time programme. You may prefer to leave work and focus full time on your studies. Although you may already have a degree it might not be appropriate for you to undertake the postgraduate route and therefore you could apply to an undergraduate programme for your study. In making the decision it is worth reflecting on your reason for undertaking the programme: are you motivated more by the achievement of a qualification or by the training you will undertake to become an occupational therapist? This may serve as the final factor in the decision-making process.

Postgraduate or undergraduate?

This may be a dilemma for a number of students who already hold a postgraduate qualification. There are over a dozen programmes across the UK, from Eastbourne to Edinburgh, offering postgraduate opportunities. These have been designed to provide an accelerated route through the required training in order that an individual can more quickly practise as a qualified and registered occupational therapist. These courses have all been accredited or approved by the College of Occupational Therapists and the Health and Care Professions Council and meet the rigorous standards required of these organisations. This route may not, however, meet the needs of everyone.

Due to the nature of these programmes the traditional student vacations may be reduced in order to create additional study time in the two years to achieve all the required objectives. This would result in students having only short periods out of study where they might reflect and re-energise.

This route might also be particularly challenging where a student takes time to settle in a new context. By their nature these programmes assume prior study skills and will encourage the student to draw upon them. There will be little by way of induction to university skills and you will be expected to begin the programme ready to learn. While you will not be expected to have prior knowledge regarding occupational therapy theory and practice there will be an assumption that you will quickly and earnestly engage in self-directed study to develop that understanding. Teaching strategies have been developed to support a more mature approach to learning. More autonomy will be expected and there will be an assumption that you will have greater motivation and self-discipline.

With these expectations you may feel it would be more appropriate that you undertake the undergraduate route to occupational therapy. This will not diminish your employment opportunities but will give you more time to process the new learning and make sense of the information you are required to handle. This may be particularly true for those graduates who are entering occupational therapy from an unrelated field. While you will bring many transferable skills to a postgraduate programme, there may be a lot of new information which needs to be understood while being able to work academically at Master's rather than undergraduate level.

Ultimately this comes down to a personal decision. You know what your work capabilities are and what you might be able to achieve. You may have plans for the future that require an accelerated training. You may have children or other family commitments which would be more problematic in either of the routes available. Only you can determine the course you wish to pursue. If you have any doubts discuss this with the admissions tutors, listen to their advice and then draw your own conclusion.

Case study: The BSc (Honours) programme – Ciaran Wilkinson

'I am currently studying in my third year on the BSc (Hons) Occupational Therapy programme at Teesside University. Over the three years I feel I have learnt a lot about the role of Occupational Therapists in different settings and what makes them different to other professions. The programme was split into numerous modules covering anatomy, psychology and sociology through to setting up businesses linked to occupational therapy. The programme modules cover a wide range of occupational therapy related subjects which have been built on over the years to allow students to develop an in-depth knowledge of the profession.

I have thoroughly enjoyed the whole programme. Every module has linked in with another part of the programme or with the practice placements. I have had varied placements, working in elderly rehabilitation and psychosis as well as learning disabilities and social services. During the placements educators both onsite and at university have provided a variety of learning experiences using different learning styles. I have found this especially beneficial as I learn by reading as well as practising. The use of seminars taught alongside the lectures has allowed me to explore the subject areas in greater depth, improving my understanding. I feel this programme has improved my skills in a number of areas and taught me how to be an occupational therapist, which I look forward to using as a professional soon.'

Case study: An MSc programme – Almaz Zakaryas

'Following my undergraduate Psychology degree, I had thought hard about the route I would pursue. I desired a profession which was diverse, purposeful and practical. Occupational therapy seemed to match my desires; the course also offered a balance between theoretical and practical work, which reinforced my learning. The Master's course provided me with an accelerated route to becoming an occupational therapist, allowing me to qualify sooner. Another advantage was that I could use my undergraduate degree, as well as my prior work and life experiences to support my educational development. Although the course would take up a lot of my time because it condensed the undergraduate degree into two years, I felt prepared for this level of commitment as I already had experience working full time. The independent learning nature of the MSc course was also accessible, as I had already gained this experience in completing an undergraduate degree. Looking back, I am sure that I began the MSc at the right time for myself, as my prior experiences have definitely influenced me as a therapist, and without those experiences I would not be the therapist I feel I am becoming now.'

Should I worry about reputation?

Every year there are a variety of league tables published which indicate that one university is better than another. The problem with league tables is that they do not always measure the things which you as a student are interested in, nor do they give a true picture of the course you are intending to study. The difficulty that you have, therefore, is determining from this information what is important to you. Certainly, a review of some of the major newspapers will highlight some significant and rigorous data. These league tables consider issues such as staff : student ratios, teaching quality, the quality of research and entry tariff points, but they represent the whole university and not necessarily the programme you are about to undertake. In 2016 in one national newspaper university league table, of the universities listed, only 2 of the top 20 has an occupational therapy programme and there were only 6 in the top 50. Yet these six programmes deliver extremely high quality training. The things which they do well may simply not be measured in the columns of the league tables. These might include student support, attrition rates or development of communication and management skills, attributes which would never be shown in a league table. It is important to understand that every programme meets the approval standards of the Health and Care Professions Council and that many programmes have received accreditation from the College of Occupational Therapists and with that accreditation they are recognised by the World Federation of Occupational Therapists.

So if you are to ignore the league tables how do you determine where to go? What may be of more value is the National Student Survey (NSS). This is an annual survey taken by the final year students of all undergraduate programmes in the UK. The survey reports on the student experience of each programme. This is not without difficulties. Different subjects are grouped together into categories and occupational therapy normally appears in 'other subjects allied to medicine'. Depending on the university, it may be the only subject in this category or it may be one of several subjects. Despite this, the results can provide some indication of the student experience. The NSS gives final year undergraduates the opportunity to provide feedback on their courses in a nationally recognised format. Students on flexible courses will be asked to participate as they near the end of their course but not necessarily in their final year. There are 23 core questions, relating to a variety of aspects of the student learning experience:

- Teaching on the course
- Assessment and feedback
- Academic support
- Organisation and management
- Learning resources
- Personal development
- Overall satisfaction
- Students' union

This data is also available with the opportunity for comparison, through the Unistats web pages. The address can be found at the end of this chapter.

Students are also given the opportunity to provide comments on their experience as a whole. While this information is forwarded to the university to help them identify how they can make improvements, it is not available to the public.

If you are considering applying to undertake a postgraduate course, the Postgraduate Taught Experience Survey will give you an idea of how postgraduate students viewed their learning experience. The results of the survey are available on the Higher Education Academy website. Postgraduate programmes are normally delivered by the same team as the undergraduate route and therefore much of the NSS data will also be reflective of all routes being delivered.

Ultimately, your choice of programme should not be based on league tables or opinions, but on your own view of what you see and experience.

If you can, go to the campus and look around. If you can meet staff, do so and get a feel for the department. If you are being interviewed remember that you are deciding if this is a suitable place for you to study. After all, you will be spending several years of your life there, if you feel uncomfortable, then it will be a very difficult experience. Make sure that the programme is delivered in a way which best meets your learning style. We will cover issues about learning styles later in this chapter.

What is the course structure?

There are a variety of different types of programme extending from two to four years. It is not practical to explore each of these individually but there are some key elements which will be found across all programmes and some things you may need to consider. These elements should be explored when considering a programme and taken into account when finally making your decision.

The starting dates of programmes differ. While most routes will commence in the autumn there are some programmes which start in January, February and April. This may have a bearing on your studies and preparation to undertake the programme. This will also have an impact on when you will complete the course and when you will be available to work. It may be an advantage to be looking for work at a time when the majority of final year students are still completing their studies.

All programmes accredited by the College of Occupational Therapists require students to successfully complete a minimum of 1,000 hours of practice placements. This gives students the opportunity to work with service users in real work situations while being supported by experienced occupational therapists. The placements will be organised in a variety of health and social care environments providing a range of learning opportunities. These placements will be interspersed throughout the programme, usually culminating in a long placement towards the end of the programme. These placements break up the time spent in the university and offer you the opportunity to apply the theory you have learned in the practice context. Chapter 8 will provide more detailed information on this aspect of your training. Occasionally some programmes teach across the traditional university vacation periods. This may mean that summer breaks are shorter or placements take you into winter or spring holiday periods.

On modular programmes you may be studying a number of modules simultaneously with assessments spread across the year or perhaps all the assessments focused into a key week or fortnight. Whichever method is used, these modules will have been organised in this way to offer the best learning experience and will have taken account of feedback from staff and students.

How do they teach and how do I learn?

For many years academics and researchers have debated the best way to teach students. While this has now tended towards the concept of lecture followed by seminar and then a tutorial, there is still much variation within and beyond this combination. As with other aspects of deciding on a university, considering which teaching methods suit you best is a matter of personal preference. The common practice is for all teaching to be divided into modules. Each module will identify and deliver certain learning outcomes which will be assessed. Modules will be of varying sizes and contain a variety of assessments proportionate to their size. Sometimes these modules may be very small ten-credit modules. Other modules are much larger representing perhaps 60 credits or more. These credits represent the number of hours spent studying a particular topic so a 60-credit module will therefore require 6 times more study time than a 10-credit module. This might be linked to a final dissertation or major project. A 10 credit module may represent 100 hours of study, but perhaps only 20 hours of this will take place in a classroom. You will be expected to complete 80 hours through self-directed study.

Some programmes will deliver the module in very short periods for example, as a block of full-time study on a single module over a week. On the plus side, this ensures you work on the material but it also means that you do not have time to reflect on your learning. Other programmes might deliver a module for two hours each week throughout the whole academic year. While this offers lots of opportunity to read and reflect on your learning, it is limited by a lack of focus and emphasis in what may be a very busy week. Your own approach to learning might fit well with either of these or a version somewhere between.

The other main strategy which is employed in teaching occupational therapy students is problem-based learning (PBL). This teaching strategy is not new, having been developed in Canada in the 1960s. It remains relatively uncommon in occupational therapy education. PBL requires students to work together in groups of about eight to resolve often complex problems. These are given in a variety of forms including paper case studies, visual, written or audio material. Students acquire subject knowledge and skills through the resolution of these problems which may have a professional context rather than working with the primary knowledge base in isolation. Teaching staff will serve as facilitators rather than tutors or lecturers, leaving students to manage the depth and breadth of learning based on their own experience, needs and expectations. Depending on the programme, PBL may be used as the basis for structuring the whole curriculum, or may be seen as a means of introducing problem-solving exercises into a traditional curriculum.

Top tip

When you attend open-days remember to ask the staff and students about the teaching styles that are used, so that you can assess whether they match your preferred learning style.

How will I be assessed?

Assessment comes in a variety of forms and each assessment on your programme will have been designed to give you the best opportunity to learn. Assessment will allow you to develop skills in preparation for your future role as an occupational therapist. It also serves to test your understanding of material and provide an objective evaluation of your progression.

While you may be familiar with or expect formal examinations these are likely to comprise only a small part of the assessment process. A variety of different assessment methods will be employed as this mix allows individual strengths to be exhibited and will make demands on a range of skills. In many cases you will be assessed in a traditional written essay format. But assessments might also include case study work, group work, presentations and the production of posters. Occasionally, there may be assessed tutorials or oral examinations. Practical skills will invariably be assessed through demonstration. Practice placements are an example of this kind of assessment, where the placement educator will assess how, for example, you carry out your treatment plans. When considering a programme of study it would be useful to enquire about the types of assessment used and consider if this suits your own learning and assessment style.

Assessment can be one of two types: summative or formative. Summative assessments are those for which you will receive a mark or grade and which will contribute to your progression and final degree classification. Formative assessment is used to inform you of your progression. You will receive feedback on all of your assessments either as a grade or as written feedback which indicates the strengths and limitations of your submitted work. Often you will receive both types of feedback. When you receive this feedback it is being provided in order that you might improve your skills and understanding. Whether you have been successful or otherwise this feedback will assist your subsequent work. It is a reflection of your work and not you and should be reviewed to inform future submissions.

Case study: Studying with dyslexia – Simon Little

'As a student with dyslexia it can be a daunting prospect when beginning studying and the best piece of advice I can offer is to embrace the services and facilities which are available. Support can come through both the university and course funding body in the form of a disabled student allowance. The latter is a fund that students can use towards assistive technology, which has greatly aided me with my studies. I personally find using a computer to make notes and review them before commencing lectures allowed me time to comprehend theory and ask questions if required. Also I find that having the opportunity to audio record lectures makes revision more manageable as I can review notes and listen to the lecture multiple times. I have had a positive experience through my studies with all academic staff being extremely accommodating to my learning needs. However, being honest, and openly discussing my individual learning style with academic tutors and practice placement educators as early as possible, meant that my learning requirements could be factored into potential learning opportunities. Disclosing your individual needs will ensure a positive learning experience and assists academic staff in understanding how best to assist where necessary. Embrace all of the support available, yet be proactive and find the best approach for you.'

Chapter summary

Whether you plan to live at home or move away, there are many aspects to take into consideration before selecting where to apply. Taking the time to study your options will help to reduce the number of surprises later, so if you really don't enjoy exams then it is wise to look closely at the assessment methods in each programme!

Assessing your academic ability in order to select the correct level of study is important too. Even if you already have a degree, you should consider both the BSc and the MSc programmes and seek the advice of the admissions tutors. Ensure you seek out learning support before starting the programme so that you can have any requirements in place.

Key points

- Check the College of Occupational Therapists website for all the available courses – choose the level of study that is best for you.
- Look at the National Student Survey and the Postgraduate Taught Experience Survey results.
- Consider the practicalities – where you will live and how far you can realistically travel.
- Check the course structure – does it suit your learning style and personal commitments?

Useful resources

College of Occupational Therapists: www.cot.co.uk

Higher Education Academy Postgraduate Taught Experience Survey: https://www.heacademy.ac.uk/research/surveys/postgraduate-taught-experience-survey-ptes

NSS results: http://unistats.direct.gov.uk/

Chapter 4

How do I apply?

BPP
UNIVERSITY
SCHOOL OF HEALTH

In this chapter we consider all of the elements of the application process. For most applicants occupational therapy is their dream profession and they will be extremely motivated to prepare their application form well.

The number of places on occupational therapy programmes differs at each university and is relatively small in comparison to other health and social care professions. Inevitably this means that competition for those places is fierce. You should take time to look at all the available programmes (you can find this information on the College of Occupational Therapists website) to ensure you are applying for the courses that suit you best. It is sensible to contact the admissions tutor to ask about the programme and whether it is possible to attend a discovery or open day as this should help you to decide which programmes to apply for.

All occupational therapy programmes require you to have a Disclosure and Barring Service (DBS) check. This will usually be an enhanced check as you will be working with children and vulnerable people. If you think that you might have something on a DBS that may preclude you from undertaking the programme you may wish to check this out with the admissions tutor before you send in your application. On an enhanced check any caution or conviction is listed, even those as a minor. Occupational Therapy programmes do have the responsibility of checking this as it would be irresponsible to train you only to find that something from your past prevented you from being able to register with the Health and Care Professions Council (the regulatory body with whom all occupational therapists must register in order to work as an occupational therapist).

The University and Colleges Admission System (UCAS)

Using the UCAS system online is the usual way to apply for Bachelor of Science with Honours (BSc (Hons)) programmes in the UK. The UCAS website has easy to follow steps with plenty of useful tips to help you through the process. The number of programmes you can apply for depends on the fee you pay. It is important that you get your application in on time, correctly completed and then track your progress using UCAS Track. It is useful to note that many universities are now using the 'gathered field' system, which means that they are waiting until all the interviews have been undertaken before offering any places. This might mean that you could wait for some considerable time before finding out if you have been successful in your application. You may wish to check with admissions tutors to see which method they are following. If you are not successful in your first applications then you may be able to apply through the UCAS Extra system or through the UCAS clearing system. If you are offered the opportunity to use UCAS Extra take the time to review your personal statement. This is because it is likely that whatever is written there has not met the criteria that admissions tutors are looking for.

Direct application

For Master of Science (MSc) programmes you will generally need to make a direct application to the university of your choice. You should be able to access and download the application forms from the individual university websites, but if not, just ring the admissions team to request that the forms are sent to you. Some universities will only have a small number of available places and may interview you and keep you on a waiting list if the places are full until the next academic year.

Case study: The application process – Erin Rolfe

'The application process was a really positive and beneficial experience for me. It gave me the opportunity to address why I had chosen to pursue a career in occupational therapy and what I could offer the profession. Having worked as an arts educator for a number of years, returning to university was a daunting prospect so having the chance to explore this decision in my application was crucial.

It was essential to reflect upon this decision as part of my application and to recognise my motivations. It was imperative to understand what the profession is, seek advice and guidance from current educators and practitioners and to gauge whether it was the right choice for me.

I spent a lot of time thinking and talking about my motivations with my family, friends and colleagues. I felt it was really helpful to break down my thinking into a number of areas including why I wanted to study again, what drew me to occupational therapy, what my motivations for following this particular career path were, what I could offer the profession and how I could benefit from the training. The application process is highly competitive so you need to take the time to really help the person who will read your application know why it is important to you and why they should consider you for interview and/or a subsequent place on the course.'

What do the admissions team look for?

Remember that not all universities are the same – you may wish to consider contacting the admissions tutor to arrange to meet with them or to chat over the phone, to get an idea of the criteria they will be using. You should refer to the information that you will find in the university prospectus and website as well as the course information that you can find on the College of Occupational Therapists website. Additionally, you may know someone who is already on the programme or you could contact current students on their Facebook page. Ask around and see what you can find out about the programme you want to undertake. One thing admissions tutors are very definitely looking for is a form that has been completed correctly!

Your form may be initially reviewed by a member of administration staff who is filtering all of the applications. This person will be checking to see that you have the correct qualifications. If you are applying from outside of the United Kingdom then it is wise to check that you have the correct qualifications before applying. A quick phone call or email to the admissions office at the university should clarify this for you.

Your personal statement

If everyone who applies has the required UCAS points and has completed the form correctly then how do admissions tutors and teams make any decisions? The best opportunity for you to demonstrate your commitment to your study and chosen profession is on the personal statement – so make sure it is something you take time to prepare. It is an opportunity to demonstrate that you are well informed about the profession and the university you are applying to.

Don't waste words relating how you first thought of doing career 'A' then changed your mind to occupational therapy. Instead, explain how the skills you have will be useful and demonstrate how you have developed those skills. Try not to base the whole statement on a story of how, for example, a member of your family was ill and an occupational therapist came to visit and you thought it looked like a fulfilling career. If you have seen an occupational therapist at work, demonstrate your understanding of what you have seen. Explain if you have been able to undertake some work experience and what you were able to learn from this. If you have attended a discovery day or an open day give an example of how this helped to confirm that occupational therapy was the career for you. Remember to cover aspects like teamwork, communication and leadership. Try to help the admissions tutor imagine you on their programme.

Case study: The admissions process – Simon Fox

'I would advise anyone seeking to study occupational therapy to do their research first. Read around the subject in order to gain a perspective on what occupational therapy is, what it entails, and what personal attributes you should have that you could bring to the profession.

Preparation and initiative is key and will give a person the edge over other prospective students who want to study occupational therapy. It is a good idea to get familiar with the field through work experience or by getting a job in the health or social care sector.

When it comes to the personal statement, it is important not to forget prior experience and the aspects of your personality that would make you a great occupational therapist. Present the personal statement in a clear and concise fashion.

For an interview, research the route to the university and give it a 'dry run' if possible, allowing plenty of time to get there on the day. First impressions count, particularly in interviews, so I would advise you to dress smartly, make eye contact and smile. An interview is a chance to promote yourself, whilst being careful to listen to others and not talk over them.'

A careers adviser may be able to help you to use a variety of expressive verbs to demonstrate your ability, rather than you using the same word over and over again. Type your personal statement in a Word document first, check the spelling and grammar and make sure it isn't repetitive. Ask someone else to read it through and give you some feedback – if your statement makes them interested then that is a good start.

The interview process

Not all universities interview prospective occupational therapy students in a traditional way, so it is imperative that you make your personal statement as good as it can be, because you may or may not get a place purely on what is written there. The interviews come in different forms – with no two universities doing the same thing. Some universities may conduct a traditional interview, some offer an interview plus some group activities and others just conduct group and individual activities, designed to find out about your skills in practice. You may find that occupational therapists from practice and service users are also involved in the process.

Individual interviews

Some people really enjoy interviews as it gives them the opportunity to sell themselves and demonstrate verbally how they feel they will be successful. Remember that the people interviewing you are not trying to find out that you know all about occupational therapy and they are certainly not trying to trip you up or make you feel incompetent. They are trying to find out what makes you the person you are, what sort of values you have and whether you have an enquiring mind. They will be asking questions to see whether you think quickly and creatively and to find out how you view the world around you.

Group interviews

The size of the group you might be in will vary and there will usually be at least two staff members there. The purpose of a group interview is to see how you interact with your fellow interviewees – do you contribute to the discussion? Are you silent throughout? Do you take over and prevent others from speaking? Do you listen to what others are saying? Are you able to challenge in an assertive way or do you let others get their own way? Do you look interested in what is going on around you or does it look like you'd rather be somewhere else? You will need to be conscious of your non-verbal behaviours as well as your verbal contribution. Remember to be your own person; don't just follow the rest – especially if you have a different view.

Top tips – Interview advice

- Plan your travel arrangements and try to arrive with time to spare.
- Wear something smart but comfortable.
- Avoid too much make up and jewellery and avoid fiddling with scarves.
- Take certificates and any other useful evidence of your achievements with you in an appropriate, tidy, clean file.
- Make sure you are sitting in a comfortable position – try not to fidget.
- Make good eye contact with the people who are interviewing you.
- Ask to have a question repeated if you don't understand it or need more time – no one is trying to trick you.
- Make sure you answer the question – give an example to help show your competence or understanding.
- Ask some sensible questions at the end of your interview.
- If you don't feel you have had the opportunity to tell the panel something significant about yourself then tell them at the end.
- Leave the panel with a really positive image of you.
- **Smile!**

Group activities

Some programmes may ask you to participate in other activities at your interview. These could be team tasks or even demonstrating how you would make a concise summary of a series of paragraphs from a book or an article. The reason for undertaking these tasks is to give you an opportunity to demonstrate how you work within a team or to show how you are able to read and understand the important points from a passage in a short period of time.

There are many practical skills which a prospective occupational therapy student would benefit from having – these are sometimes difficult to convey on an application form, therefore the admissions team is offering you the chance to demonstrate them – so try not to get too anxious. Again, no one is trying to catch you out; try to relax and do your best.

It is important for you to know that in devising the application and interview process, many universities have consulted service users and carers, as well as employers, to see what sort of characteristics they all feel are important for occupational therapy students to have. This isn't just about academic ability – you need to be an all-rounder. So if service users and carers have said that it is important for occupational therapists to demonstrate good listening skills it will be important for you to demonstrate this in your interview or activity. Employers may say that assertiveness is a key skill – so you'll need to show that too. Try to imagine the skills and personal attributes that you would value in a healthcare professional working with you, then assess if you can demonstrate those skills in your interview.

Case study: Service users involvement in the admissions process – Janet Walker

'One of my first roles at the university as a service user was that of assisting in interviewing candidates for places on the occupational therapy programmes.

The thing I found most interesting about being involved in the interview process was the way in which it was structured.

Candidates were assessed over a two hour period, taking part in a group discussion, individual practical activities and having one to one discussions with the three different interviewers, of which I was one.

It was interesting to observe different attitudes and responses from the candidates. I felt the interview process was less formal and less intimidating than individual interviews would have been.

In deciding who to offer places to it was interesting to listen to the other interviewers' views and opinions. I was made to feel that my opinions mattered and felt valued and part of a team.'

Feedback

If you have attended an interview and are not fortunate enough to be offered a place, it is important to contact the university and ask if it would be possible to have some feedback about your performance. This might feel uncomfortable at first, but it is a valuable way to find out how well you did and to get some information to help improve your performance in future. When you make the telephone call, ensure you have paper and a pen to hand so you can jot down the constructive feedback that you should be given. Try not to be defensive about it – remember that other people may not see you as you see yourself. They are giving you honest feedback in the hope that it will be useful to you.

> *'When I wasn't successful at my first interview I contacted the university to ask for feedback. I was nervous and unsure what they would say, but the feedback I was given was very useful. I didn't realise that my eye contact had been at the floor rather than at the interview panel and that I had given very brief answers. The tutor advised me to give examples when I answered the questions too. I followed the feedback and felt more confident at my next interview, which must have come across to the panel as I was offered a place.'*

You might choose to work on the feedback by yourself or you could consider taking the feedback to your careers adviser, personal tutor or a friend and work through the points with them. It might be helpful to undertake a practice interview to build up your skills too. This could be with a family member or a friend.

What if I still have questions?

It is good to have questions about the programme and there are several ways to find out the answers. General questions about occupational therapy can be answered by the student officer at the College of Occupational Therapists. You can contact them via the website. Specific questions about the individual occupational therapy programmes can be answered by the admissions tutor. These people are usually contactable by telephone or email, and you will be able to find their contact details on the university website. Don't be afraid to ask your question – if you need to know something then others may too, and it will help the universities when they review the information they provide for prospective students. You might want to follow occupational therapists on Facebook or Twitter. As well as following the College of Occupational Therapists and the World Federation of Occupational Therapists you will be able to find many individual occupational therapists on either of these two social networking sites. You will also find the student occupational therapy groups for lots of universities, both in the UK and abroad. You can post questions and you'll find that students are happy to tell you the answers about their own university. You might want to know about how students formally evaluate occupational therapy programmes and you will find this out if you look at the National Student Survey and the Postgraduate Taught Experience Survey results.

So, hopefully you are now ready to start to prepare your application. Remember to leave sufficient time to research your chosen course and complete the forms, as your future career could depend on how thorough you are at this stage.

Chapter summary

It is important to demonstrate your enthusiasm and understanding of occupational therapy on your application form. You need to stand out from the rest of the applicants, so think widely about how to link your skills and experiences to show how you are the best applicant for the place. If you are offered an interview, follow the advice given earlier in this chapter, go with a positive outlook and be yourself.

Key points

- Check your DBS status – clarify the position with the Health and Care Professions Council if you are unsure.
- Consider the practicalities – where you will live and how far you can realistically travel.
- Attend discovery days or open days – and ask questions.
- Prepare your application forms – check for spelling and grammatical errors and ensure all the required information is completed.
- Arrange a practice interview with a friend – even if you don't need one, this is a useful thing to do.
- Prepare for your interview, read some up-to-date occupational therapy literature, visit an occupational therapist at work, find something smart but comfortable to wear (and polish your shoes!).
- Plan your travel arrangements so that you arrive safely and calmly for your interview.

Useful resources

Health and Care Professions Council: www.hcpc-uk.org/

The Universities and Colleges Admissions Service: www.ucas.com

Results of the National Student Survey and Postgraduate Taught Experience Survey: http://unistats.direct.gov.uk/

Chapter 5

What is life like as a student?

BPP UNIVERSITY SCHOOL OF HEALTH

Even if you have been a college or university student before, life as an occupational therapy student, studying for a professional qualification, is quite different. This chapter contains information to help you to plan for the years of study ahead.

Accommodation

Where you are going to live as a student is a very important decision and should not be taken without thorough consideration. Whatever you choose you will have to live with it for the next few months. There are a number of options available to you. Here we will consider the main ones.

Living in student halls

Student halls are a great way to begin your time at university. These are often managed by the university and will have all the basics required for life at university. There are sometimes opportunities to have all your meals included in this package. While being more expensive than other options, there is a degree of certainty in this accommodation and parents often value the additional assurance that this may provide. You will meet lots of new people who are studying a wide range of subjects. This helps you to mix with people other than occupational therapists. Sharing a building with lots of other people will also create some difficulties as not everyone wishes to study as much as you do, sleep as much as you do or respect the privacy of others as you do. While this is rarely a problem some people will prefer to use halls only for their first year. This leaves some other considerations.

Living in a shared house

This might happen in one of two ways. The accommodation office at the university might indicate this as an option and you will be placed in a house with other students allocated to the same type of housing. This is similar in experience to student halls, but on a smaller scale. You are now self-catering and you don't have someone who comes in and cleans your room. The other approach to sharing a house often occurs during your later years of study. You get together with some friends and arrange to rent a house together, usually from a private landlord. This is often the cheapest way of living. You may be paying your own bills as well as your living costs, and this must be taken into account when you make your decision.

Renting a room

For those who are looking for a home away from home this is the choice for you. It is sometimes possible to rent a room in someone else's home. This will provide you with your own bedroom with study area and usually access to the kitchen. Occasionally you may have meals provided within the cost of the accommodation. This is often a great option as you are in someone else's home, with all the advantages of this. Bear in mind that they may not appreciate you coming in at 3.30am after socialising with your student friends and telling the whole house about it. It is, after all, their home. This type of accommodation may isolate you from the other students but may suit your personality.

There is no 'right' answer regarding which accommodation to choose. You must look for something that will be suitable for you. Contact the university accommodation office and they will be able to help you consider your options.

Finance

This will be considered in more detail in the next chapter. Being a student will usually require personal sacrifice and it will be necessary for you to adjust your finances in order to survive the budgetary restrictions which might be imposed by attending university. There is a culture of debt associated with being at university and while this is inevitable it should not be a burden nor should it be ignored. Read Chapter 6 for more information on how this might be managed.

Timetables

Your time at university is going to be managed through a timetable system. This will be very similar to the one in place at your college or school. You may be expected to attend sessions which are spread across a large campus or even on two different sites. It is not true that the timetable is constructed to make things as difficult as possible for students but it does have to fit in with the timetable of thousands of other students, staff and rooms! This will mean that occasionally a class will run during the evening or as early as 9.00am. This is a fact of life and it is your responsibility to be there. Attendance on many occupational therapy programmes is now monitored and so it is important that you do attend or you may find yourself having to explain your absences to the programme leader and in serious cases you may be asked to leave the course.

There is an expectation that you attend all youir classes. You will be studying on a skills based course and you need to be able to learn and practise all of the required skills. This provides important reassurance to your future clients. After all, you would not like to visit a hairdresser who had not attended the training sessions for cutting or colouring; you certainly would not like to be operated on by a surgeon who had only completed half of their training.

The timetable may leave you with gaps during the day of two or three hours. While this might be a little inconvenient, it also organises space in your day to meet with other students in a study group, arrange appointments with tutors or just give you time to go to the library and read quietly. It should not be seen as time wasted, but as an opportunity.

'I'd never really used a library before for formal study. I made time to meet the subject librarian and went to some sessions to find out all of the different services the library could provide. Popping in between lectures helped me to structure any free time and the librarians were so helpful when I needed special books and papers for my dissertation.'

Timetabled sessions are arranged for a particular length of time. Your lecturers will prepare material to best use that time. It will be in your interest to attend the sessions from the beginning in order that you get the most out of them. Arriving late disturbs the class, affects the flow of the session and gives others a wrong impression about you. If you know you are going to be late, do what you can to let the lecturer know. This might mean texting a friend to pass on the message or phoning the lecturer. Some programmes will not allow you into a session once it has started. This may be due to the nature of the session or just out of courtesy to the rest of the group. This may have a longer-term impact on your attendance. Always do your best to get some notes of the sessions you miss.

Books and equipment

On arrival, or perhaps before, you will be inundated with lists of things you will need. This will include a book list. These are provided to give you some indication of the range of books which should be read for your particular course of study. There are books that you have to buy, books which you have to read and books which are recommended for reading. Unfortunately, books are also very expensive and you would expect to pay between £25 and £75 for each text book on the list. However, it is not essential that you buy every book on the list and the book buying process should be as economical and relevant as possible.

When a friend recommends you read a book it is rare that you do so without considering the advertising, the reviews or the blurb. Often you will pick up the book, flick through its pages and perhaps read some of its content. This should be the same with a text book. Rarely will a text provide you with the only source of information on a topic and it may be that while you find one style of writing difficult to follow, another might explain things in a way which you connect with immediately. There are, for example, many anatomy and physiology text books, each presenting the human body in a slightly different way. The material being considered (the human body) does not change.

Top tips

- Look through several text books on the same subject before selecting any to buy.
- Up-to-date texts are in the library so you need only buy specialist books about the areas of practice you are interested in.

It may also be true that an earlier edition of a text book will have much the same material as the newest edition. The new version may present the material in a different way, have new illustrations and might use colour rather than black and white images but the material may be fundamentally the same. In these cases older editions might be bought at a reduced price or easily obtained second hand. There is often a second hand book market within the student body of the university.

At this point it should also be made clear that as the theory and practice of occupational therapy constantly changes there is a need to update text books. These theoretical developments and adaptations to practice will greatly alter the content of the text book and render previous editions educationally irrelevant except as historical documents. For this reason it is recommended that you discuss the purchase of older books with your tutor who may be familiar with the texts and will be able to offer advice.

Your programme may also require you to have certain pieces of equipment to support your studies. This may be something basic like a set of colouring pencils but they may also expect you to purchase something more expensive such as art materials or perhaps clothing. Where these can be bought second hand, this option might be considered and students further through the programme may be able to assist with this. Some items may be relevant throughout your career and this should also be taken into account.

Induction week

In many ways induction week is the most influential week of your university career. This may be called freshers' week in some institutions or by some programmes. It is usually the first week of the first university term or semester. This is a great opportunity to get to know the university, the staff and the other students with whom you will be spending the next few years of your life. It is often difficult starting out in a new environment but, remember, you will be surrounded by many others who are also making that new start. You are all experiencing this new event together. By making lots of different friends you are more likely to find the people with whom you can work effectively. Try not to become too attached to only one person during this period. While they may be great fun to have around during this introductory week they may not be the best support when things become more focused and serious later in the year.

There will be some timetabled events during this period when you will complete registrations, sign forms and receive lots of information about the programme. It is likely that you will receive your timetable and direction on the expectations and rules for the programme. The programme team will have spent many hours planning what should be included in this period so it is important that you attend all sessions.

This period is also the time when there will be lots of additional activities happening across the university. Local business will be trying to attract your custom and may be tempting you with great offers, including free pizza, discounted driving lessons or half price entry. It is sometimes easy to get carried away with all the hustle and bustle of these events. Think carefully before committing yourself to any of these offers. You can always collect the information and go back to them in two weeks when you have had time to think about it.

> *'Even though I was living at home while I was at university, I still felt it was important to go to the events at freshers' week. I joined the occupational therapy society and the drama society. At the end of my programme I was able to add membership of these societies to my curriculum vitae too.'*

The other aspect of freshers' week to consider is the parties. They are on every night and all night if you read all the flyers you will be given. This is only one week and your finances need to last the year so be wary of spending the next month's rent on one great night. Enjoy yourself but remain in control.

Library facilities

Using the library is one of the most essential skills you need to learn during your studies. When you watch the television quiz *University Challenge* the contestants introduce themselves by indicating they are 'reading' their subject area. This is not said by accident. There is awareness that in order to learn about your subject you need to read about it. The best place for this to happen is in your library. What is great about modern libraries is that they do not consist only of dusty books filling hundreds of shelves; they also have access to millions of electronically published articles. They will also let you access these articles from your own home (although you will need the internet and you do need to follow some rules). Just imagine, you can read almost every article written on occupational therapy without leaving your desk (or even your bed but that might give the wrong message!). These articles are usually published in professional magazines called journals, which are also made accessible over the internet. Journals provide you with the most-up-to date information within your academic discipline or profession. Libraries have traditionally held stocks of these journals going back many years and bound together in volumes. Each volume usually contains a year of journals.

In relation to your studies the journals are supported by text books. You will probably be familiar with these. Text books provide an alternative source of information. Unlike journals, a text book can be borrowed from the library. You may be able to borrow ten or more books at a time depending on the policy of the library. The library will never have enough books for every student to have their own copy of every text book so you should seriously consider buying the key text books for yourself or, even better, ask someone else to buy one for you. In order to increase access to text books, libraries are increasingly subscribing to e-books. This gives students electronic access to the content of text books without having to physically hold it. It also means that students can access these books more readily.

The library may also have stocks of video clips, television programmes, and music. They will certainly receive the major daily newspapers which give you alternative learning resources. The only way you can get the most out of this is to familiarise yourself with the library as soon as you can. The library will probably run sessions on how to make use of its resources. Get signed up for these early in your programme and find out what to do before you have to prepare your first assignment.

University support

All universities invest a lot of resources to ensure that students have the most enjoyable and successful experience possible. There is a range of student support services available to try to ensure that students maximise their potential. As students come from a wide variety of backgrounds with a range of life experiences, each brings their own perspective. Your experiences will be very different to those around you and therefore, your needs will differ. A university needs to have these services in place to support all their students. It is good to make yourself aware of the potential support on offer in order that you know where to seek help when it is needed. This section will consider a range of services but these will vary from institution to institution.

Academic support

Writing for university can be quite daunting. You may not have experience of working at this level and the university will often have a department which will help you as you try to write your assignments. This may be about constructing your essays, writing in the third person (this is usual practice for most assignments) or perhaps interpreting the questions effectively. They may offer direction to you or perhaps help by proofreading some of your work. While this service does play a key role, remember that your personal tutor or the module team are the best people to discuss your assignments with.

Financial support

While this will be considered in more detail in Chapter 6, remember that the university can only offer support in very limited ways. The university will be able to offer lots of advice to students having financial difficulty. Finance advisers will be available throughout the year to give you advice and information on money matters. This may be about tuition fees, grants, student loans or welfare benefits. The student support team will be able to offer guidance and help with any difficulties which arise.

Student services can also help you to apply to the funding schemes they administer, such as the Access to Learning Fund. The Access to Learning Fund can provide extra help if you're in hardship and need extra financial support. Your university or college will look at your individual circumstances and may be able to help with course or living costs that are not already covered by other forms of financial help – these could be everyday living costs, childcare costs or support over the summer period, for emergency payments to cover unexpected financial crises or if you are thinking of giving up your course because of financial problems and need extra support to help you keep studying.

Counselling services

Sometimes being away from home, working in a new environment and being put under pressure can be very difficult to cope with. Without the local support of a family and perhaps not having formed strong friendships, this can become more challenging. There is sometimes a concern that expressing doubts and reflecting on personal problems might influence others' attitudes, making some issues too difficult to discuss with a personal tutor. Student support services will provide the opportunity to speak privately with a trained counsellor. This might be used for any aspect of your life and not just the academic demands. As these services are private the course team will generally have no knowledge of this support unless you wish to disclose it. As with any aspects of your personal life which might impact on your studies, it is advisable that this be mentioned, if not discussed with your personal tutor. This will ensure that you receive the best possible support throughout your studies.

Personal tutors

A personal tutor is the university's attempt to provide you with a best friend. This may sound a little trite but if we look at what they do, you will see why it is crucial to spend time with them. In ideal circumstances you will be assigned a personal tutor during induction week. They will still be working with you until after you leave, as they will also provide you with your references when you finally start being interviewed for jobs.

For many students you will be leaving home for the first time, and you will be trying to manage yourself for the first time. It is not always convenient or appropriate to speak to someone at home, and they would not necessarily appreciate what university means. This is where your tutor fits in. Whether you are 18 or 58, your tutor will take an interest in your academic development. This might be informally with some occasional discussions about your progress when you or they feel it appropriate. They may wish to formalise this process. This might include a range of meetings throughout the period of your training either as individual one to one sessions or as part of a group of tutees. These meetings will be used to support your academic and personal development while at university. Sometimes these sessions will be used to feed into your personal development portfolio. You may discuss your achievements and the opportunities available to you. You can work together on strategies to make the most of these resources, developing targets and the action plans necessary to achieve them.

Case study: The benefits of a personal tutorial – Shaun Armstrong

'In my experience I believe personal tutorials to be an integral part of the occupational therapy course as through them I have been able to develop myself as a person and increase my confidence when going out on placement. It is an informal meeting where I am able to ask questions about the course, assignments, the modules or any general questions about occupational therapy, and to be open and honest about my progress without feeling under pressure. Sometimes university can be overwhelming and you just need to express openly about an issue; using a personal tutorial allows you to reflect upon this in a non-judgemental environment. Tutorials are also a great way to build rapport with the academic staff. I feel that by utilising personal tutorials effectively it has allowed me to develop my understanding of the importance of what it means to be an occupational therapist and where I want to develop myself in the future. I consider my personal tutorials to be a major contributing factor in my path to becoming a successful occupational therapist therefore I always ensure I turn up fully prepared, as failing to prepare is preparing to fail.'

Where things are not working well your tutor will also help you to reflect on the experience and consider ways to improve your situation. Remember that your tutor knows about university and its organisation and routines. They understand the student support services and how to read a timetable.

You also need to be aware that your tutor will have other roles. It is not sufficient to turn up at their door and expect half an hour of their time. It may be that you have to email them first or set up a tutorial appointment in order that you can have their full attention. It may be necessary to give them some indication of the nature of your appointment. This will allow your tutor to prepare for the meeting and perhaps book an alternative room to ensure you have privacy. You may also be expected to prepare material for your meeting. You will only get the best out of your tutor if you invest the effort. Having your tutor on your side will certainly make the university experience easier.

Extra-curricular activities

Academic work will take up a large part of your time at university and you should recognise this. This does not, however, prevent you from being involved in other activities or taking on new responsibilities. For some students there will be ongoing family responsibilities which will take precedence over anything else. For many students this will be a time of many new starts. As you make decisions about what you want to do with your time outside of your studies bear in mind that the academic year will have periods when your workload will greatly increase.

Part-time work is often a consideration for students. While this is not the ideal situation when studying, it is realistic to acknowledge the necessity of additional income. Bearing this in mind, any potential employer may need to be very flexible. While the timetable may be relatively fixed from week to week, the introduction of your practice placements will commit you to full-time work for a fixed term with the potential for increased travel time. You will also be expected to carry out additional reading or complete projects or presentations which may consume much of your evenings or weekends. This may have an impact on your employment and may need early discussion to avoid longer-term problems.

The students' union and the BAOT subgroup

There are hundreds of students' unions across the country. They are all members of the National Union of Students (NUS). The students' union at your university is there to represent you. It looks after the needs of students in many different ways. In order to get the most out of the union you need to learn more about it, how it can help you and how you can get more involved in running the union yourself. The union exists to improve your experience of university life. It provides welfare services and entertainment such as clubs and bars. Many will also have shops or catering outlets where snacks can be purchased.

Many groups need to have a national voice to ensure there is full representation. The NUS exists to promote, defend and extend the rights of students (NUS, 2012). It fights and campaigns for change with student interests at heart. The union also works on a local level to provide representation for students. This might be through course and faculty representatives; students trained to represent their cohort who meet formally with senior staff from the university to review the programmes and the student experience. They may also flag up unresolved or ongoing issues to university representatives. The union may also offer advisers who can provide independent, professional advice to students when they are having academic problems and where necessary support them in disciplinary hearings held by the university.

The NUS also offers you the NUS extra discount card. For a low annual fee this offers a range of discounts, deals and competitions designed to make student life a little more rewarding. You can use it to make your money go further on books, clothes, sports stuff, CDs, travel, computer gear, gigs, eating out etc. This can also be converted to a PASS card for an additional fee. PASS is the government accredited scheme for proof of age which works alongside passport and driving licences. Any money spent in the students' union will be put back into student services and helps make the place better for you.

The union also oversees the organisation and management of a number of student societies. These exist to provide opportunities for students to develop new or maintain current hobbies and skills. This might include anything from religious groups to role playing games, from sports to study. You may find your university also includes an occupational therapy society. This will be open to any student in the university and will exist to provide additional learning or social opportunities specifically for the OT members of the society. This society may also be affiliated to the College of Occupational Therapists as a British Association of Occupational Therapists (BAOT) sub-group.

You will need to become a member to take full advantage of the sub-group. Setting up your BAOT student membership is quick and simple. It will take you around ten minutes to complete the documentation. Even if you do not need to pay for your membership, you still need to activate your membership on the College of Occupational Therapists website to access the resources. Student membership will give you access to a wide range of resources which will help you in your assignments and preparing for practice placements. Being a student member will keep you updated on professional issues. You can also get involved in professional development opportunities that enhance your CV, such as attending events or writing an article for publication.

Due to the way your training is funded, you may need to pay for your BAOT student membership yourself. Others will have their membership paid by their university. The student membership fee is paid monthly and current details can be found on the College of Occupational Therapists website.

Case study: Being a member of BAOT and the OT Society – Caroline Robinson

'Becoming a student member of the BAOT/COT has been vital to my learning and personal development while studying occupational therapy. First, it gave me access to a range of journals, printed and online, which proved invaluable when writing assignments and, as the BAOT resources are student friendly, I could easily develop my understanding of theories, contemporary issues and research. Membership entitles students to attend training sessions and conferences enabling greater networking and personal development, vastly enriching their professional portfolio.

Personally, I believe that student-run occupational therapy societies can be especially beneficial allowing involvement throughout a university career. For myself, I was able to further develop leadership, communication and organisational skills through arranging seminars and events offering a chance to expand members' knowledge of clinical areas not experienced through clinical placements, with CPD certificates to add to their portfolios. These skills are not individual to the committee as society members are also encouraged to approach professionals and organise events to benefit the entire society. Finally, I believe a society breaks down barriers between different cohorts and programmes (BSc and MSc) encouraging socialising and networking prospects.'

Chapter summary

Whether this is your first time at university or whether you are returning to complete another degree, it is always important to be prepared as this should help to give you confidence and reduce stress. There are so many different ways to get support while you study and you will find that rather than being aloof and unapproachable, your lecturers are eager to help you to learn and understand. You just need to let them know that you require some help. Joining your professional body, getting involved in local and national professional events and pacing yourself with your extra-curricular activities will all help make your university years a success.

Key points

- Plan a personal study timetable – if you stick to it this should reduce your stress levels later.
- Don't rush out and buy all the books on the reading list – check first with your personal tutor or the students who are already on the programme.
- Join The British Association of Occupational Therapists (BAOT).
- Go steady in induction week – there is a lot of time left to pay for!
- Make time to learn how the library works and how to get the most from it.
- If you must take on a part-time job ensure your employer understands that you will need time to undertake your practice placements.

Useful resources

Joining BAOT as a student member: www.cot.co.uk/join-baot/become-student-member

National Union of Students: www.nus.org.uk/

Student finance and the Access to Learning Fund: www.direct.gov.uk/en/EducationAndLearning/UniversityAndHigherEducation/StudentFinance/index.htm

Reference

NUS (2012) *About NUS.* [Online] Available at: www.nus.org.uk/en/about-nus/ [Accessed 27 May 2016].

Chapter 6

How do I manage my finances as a student?

BPP UNIVERSITY SCHOOL OF HEALTH

A significant issue for individuals considering higher education study is the cost of a chosen programme of study. The decision to begin a university programme will likely create a situation of debt which you may never have experienced and which you may not be comfortable with. The questions that many potential occupational therapists ask are, 'How will I afford my training?', 'What will I do if I can't pay for the basics like food and rent?' and 'How can I afford a social life?' Managing your money is an essential part of university life. By making sure your costs are covered you will reduce the risk of getting into financial difficulties later on. Whether you have supported yourself financially for many years, or you're moving out of home for the first time there are a number of things you might be able to take into account to ensure a degree of financial stability. Most financial advisers will encourage you to use a budget planner to help you budget – good money management will make your student finances last longer and university life less stressful. By considering the ideas presented in this chapter, you may find it easier to support yourself during the course without leaving university with a large burden of debt.

Managing your money during your training is essential. Although there are obvious costs such as accommodation and food there are many others such as: travel, insurance, text books or equipment, bills and leisure activities. You should take time to consider what it is you need, how much it will be, and how you will pay for it. Any budget will consider a number of elements.

The total income you expect to receive or savings you can use during the academic year including:

- Savings
- Student loan
- Grants or bursaries
- Income from a job

The details of the essential items you expect to spend your money on including:

- Rent
- Travel
- Insurance
- Car bills
- Credit card payments
- Utility bills, for example, water, gas, electricity, if applicable
- Phone bills and internet
- TV licence and TV packages
- Food and drink
- Laundry costs
- Council Tax

Once the essential outgoings have been subtracted from the income you can more easily see what money you have left for the extras such as:

- Course books and equipment
- Household goods
- Clothes/shoes
- Toiletries
- Music/films
- Social activities

There will be additional costs subject to your own personal circumstances.

'I wasn't so careful with my money in the first term and this caused me problems throughout the rest of that year. My personal tutor pointed me in the direction of student services, where there was a financial adviser who helped me to sort out my money, which helped reduce my stress. I didn't realise how much money I spent on things I didn't need.'

Top tip

The UCAS budget calculator is one of a number of budget calculators available to use in planning your finances. The link can be found at the end of the chapter.

This chapter will now look in detail at some of the key aspects of finance while studying.

Accommodation costs

University accommodation costs vary greatly across the country and are dependent on factors such as geography and the level of facilities provided. Private accommodation is usually the cheapest form of accommodation but is also often of the lowest standard. Universities tend to offer self-catered and catered accommodation which can be more expensive but provide greater quality accommodation. Gas and electricity costs, and rates are all included in the overall charge for university accommodation whereas these may have to be paid for separately if you rent privately. Once you leave home you will also have to consider protecting your possessions, so it is important that you insure your property. As you do not own the property you rent it is unnecessary to obtain buildings insurance. You can choose what to cover, such as clothes, TV and phone and the cost depends on where you are living and what you insure. You can also ask for cover for when you are away from your accommodation for example if you take your laptop out with you. If you will be living in halls of residence, speak to your accommodation office about their insurance policy.

As a student living in university accommodation you will be exempt from Council Tax. This is also true if you are living in a property which is occupied solely by students. If you are a full-time student and you live with others who are not students then the house will be liable for Council Tax. Your student status may allow the household to get a discount (or an exemption) depending on individual circumstances. Additional information can be found on the Directgov website or from your local council. You will need evidence from your university in order to confirm your student status.

Are there professional costs related to my course?

There are likely to be some additional costs related to your programme of study. How much you pay will depend on you and the programme selected. Membership of the British Association of Occupational Therapists is one of the costs that you will need to meet. Due to the way some programmes are funded they may pay for this on your behalf. Where this is not the case you will need to meet this cost yourself. In 2016 these fees were only £7.41 for the month. It is not essential that you take on this membership but it is an expectation of your university that you do so and there are many benefits of being a member. Aside from this, there are no other professional costs which all students would be expected to pay.

Individual programmes may introduce additional costs related to the actual programme delivered. This might be to cover materials used in teaching sessions or for extra-curricular learning opportunities. These costs are likely to be kept to a minimum and will not have been applied without careful consideration.

Although not technically a professional cost, another cost related to your studies will be in relation to the library. When books are not returned on time there will be fines to pay. These can quickly mount up, so it is worthwhile making sure you only take out the books you need and are likely to use within the period of the loan. Another cost relating to the library is the cost of photocopying, whether this is copying journal articles or pages from books. Although a copy might only be a few pence this will soon mount up; ten articles of six to seven pages in length will be a few pounds. It is more economical for you to scan the articles and email the scanned document to yourself. This can then be stored on your own computer for access whenever you need it, rather than having to search for a hard copy that you might have mislaid, or perhaps, more frustratingly for a single page which has been lost. Depending on the university you attend, you may also have to print out each assignment to submit a paper copy. In addition, you may need to print and bind two copies of the final project or dissertation. You will need to factor in the cost of paper and printer cartridges if you are using your own printer. It is worth remembering that most universities will not allow you to graduate until all of your university accounts (such as course fees, library fines and photocopying bills) have been paid.

Where you can, try to keep costs low, but do not mistake saving money for efficiency as the benefits may be essential to your professional development.

Will I have to pay fees?

From August 2017 new occupational therapy students in England will be required to pay for their own training and university fees. This will be funded through tuition and maintenance loans. This decision will have an impact on training in other areas of the United Kingdom.

Can I obtain a student loan?

This section is not intended to encourage you to take on a loan nor to indicate any preference for a loan or its provider. There are a variety of different loans which a student might be able to access and some of these may be accessible to only some students depending on circumstances.

You will be able to apply for the standard student support system provided by the Student Loans Company to cover the cost of your tuition fees and means tested support for living costs. Loan repayments will be the same as those on other non-NHS degree programmes. This means that repayment will start once a graduate is earning £21,000 and repayments are 9% of income over that threshold. This means that a newly qualified band 5 occupational therapist earning £22,000 will pay back approximately £7.50 per month. If the loan has not been paid back after 30 years then the remainder of the loan is written off.

There are two types of loan offered. Tuition fee loans lend up to £9,000 paid directly to the course provider on your behalf. These payments are staged over the year based upon your continuation with the programme. This loan need not be paid until after you have completed the course and in work.

Maintenance loans are also available and these are applied for in the same way. Funds are loaned at the beginning of the term and are means tested subject to your own particular circumstances. This will differ according to whether you are at home or away from home and whether you are living in London or not.

Students on the preregistration Masters courses will also be able to apply for a postgraduate masters loan. Students can borrow up to £10,000 over the duration of the course to use towards their fees and living costs. As with the other loans, the repayments commence when the £21,000 earnings threshold has been reached. Repayments will be at 6% of income above the threshold and repayments are made alongside repayments of outstanding undergraduate student loans.

In addition to the loans available, students with adult or child dependants can apply for additional funding in the form of an allowance awarded according to individual circumstances.

A Professional and Career Development Loan may suit your purposes. This might be used to pay for learning that enhances your job skills or career prospects. It can be used for living expenses or to buy books or equipment. This is still a bank loan but the interest on the loan is suspended until one month after the end of your programme. The details for this can be found on the Directgov website.

Case study: Working whilst studying – Kimberley Stevenson

'Completing the MSc Occupational Therapy (pre-registration) course whilst working part time can, at times, be both challenging and stressful. The course requires a substantial amount of independent study time which initially made me apprehensive to commit to additional work responsibilities. However, as a student having to fund myself using only my savings account and student bursary, whilst living away from home, it became a necessity for me to seek part-time work in order to fund my everyday living. As the timetable at university usually requires my attendance twice a week, I felt that this was achievable. Nevertheless, this part-time work brings with it increased tiredness and less time available to focus on my studies.

Due to the course timetable changing in each term, I needed to find a job that was flexible in terms of shift patterns and attendance to allow me to work around the course. I made the decision not to work during placement time, as this is an already demanding period which requires attendance 37.5 hours per week alone. I find that working ten hours per week during the university period is just enough to support me financially without having a negative impact on my studies. I sacrifice leisure time during the weekend and on weekday evenings to engage in the independent study time that is required and necessary for the course.'

Special needs funding application

If you have a recognised special learning need, perhaps because you have a diagnosis of dyslexia or other disability, then you should ensure that you apply for the funding and support that you are entitled to. Some students do not realise that they have a special need until they have been studying for a while and had some feedback from their tutors. You can still apply for this funding after you have started your programme of study. The support you get depends on your individual needs and not on income. The allowance can help with things such as the cost of specialist equipment or additional travel costs. This is available through the gov.uk website or there may be some funding available through your university.

This may be something you are aware of and can be declared in your application. You may also discuss it with the student support services at the university when you have a confirmed offer of a place. The earlier this is discussed, the more likely it will be that appropriate support and provision will be in place at the beginning of your training.

Case study: Special needs funding – Matt

'I knew I had dyslexia but didn't realise I could apply for extra funding because of this. With the money I received I bought an iPad so that I could easily make notes and record the lectures as they happened. I got lots of practical help too, and the combination of funding and support really made a difference to my ability to study successfully.'

Chapter summary

Whatever your situation, you will need to have sufficient funds to see you through your time at university. There are some decisions to make about whether to apply for a student loan or perhaps to get a part-time job to supplement your income. There are positive and negative sides to each and it is recommended that you seek financial advice before making any decisions. As well as the funding opportunities already discussed in this chapter, you may be able to secure sponsorship from charities or even the large supermarkets. Some big organisations have sponsorship schemes so it is always worthwhile researching the possibilities and making an application. Remember that banks will also give you student bank accounts, with a variety of incentives for you to choose from. Other student benefits may include (depending on eligibility) free dental treatment and reduced Council Tax. Finally, joining the National Union of Students will allow you to get discounts for admission to films, theatre, National Trust properties and many more places. You'll also get a discount in many stores – which is a bonus especially at Christmas!

Key points

- Learn how to budget effectively.
- Plan an annual and full course budget.
- Identify potential sources of support before you have financial difficulties.

Useful resources

Student finance: www.gov.uk/browse/education/student-finance

Disabled student's allowances: www.gov.uk/disabled-students-allowances-dsas/how-to-claim

UCAS budget calculator: www.ucas.com/ucas/undergraduate/finance-and-support/budget-calculator

Chapter 7

What do the early years of studying occupational therapy involve?

BPP UNIVERSITY SCHOOL OF HEALTH

Whenever you commence new studies there will be some anxiety regarding what will be involved and what is expected of you. This is natural and any teaching team will be well placed to acknowledge your concerns and support you throughout the experience. All occupational therapy programmes throughout the United Kingdom follow the same curriculum guidelines and have been approved and accredited by representatives of both the Health and Care Professions Council and the College of Occupational Therapists. This ensures all programmes deliver material of the highest standards, but which is ultimately similar. The difference between programmes is the manner in which that material is organised and delivered. This will be adapted to the interests and the expertise of the teaching team or the facilities available at the university. The course will also be tailored to fully exploit the social and regional context of the programme and the university.

Your programme of studies will have been specifically designed so that you gain the most from the experience. It will be organised to ensure that the things you learn early in the programme will be used as a basis for future learning. This is an essential aspect of higher education and has been developed through many years of teaching and educational research. Your first year will provide you with opportunities to learn more about yourself as well as the profession. You will have opportunities to reflect on your own strengths and the areas in which you feel you could improve. You will also learn what you can achieve and how you might do so. The teaching team will provide you with a range of opportunities to develop your understanding of what occupational therapy is and how occupational therapists view the world. Your programme will allow you to develop an understanding of primary theories before being asked to apply them in more complex situations. The exception to this is problem-based learning which we have already discussed in Chapter 3.

This chapter will explore some key elements that are frequently delivered in the first year of an occupational therapy programme and will explain some key strategies you could employ to make the most of the learning opportunities.

What skills can I transfer to the programme?

Everyone will enter the programme with some type of formal qualification. A Levels (or their equivalent), an access course or a previous degree will have already developed your study skills which will be very important as you progress through your occupational therapy training.

You will also come to your occupational therapy studies with a range of personal attributes and skills which you have developed throughout your life. It may be that you enjoy helping people and solving problems. Perhaps you are patient, practical, creative and a good communicator and you might want to help people optimise their quality of life. These attributes might have been demonstrated when you applied to university through your personal statement or during the interview process. These skills are highly valued alongside your academic skills.

Because occupational therapists work across a wide range of settings there will be opportunities for you to apply some of your personal skills and your previous experience within the university based programme as well as during your practice placements. These personal attributes enrich the learning experiences of others and will be viewed as being important on the course and welcomed by staff. Your experiences are valuable and help others to understand the world in which we live, and you will learn important information through the insight of others.

> *'I came to the occupational therapy programme from a previous career in hairdressing. I was unsure which skills I could possibly transfer from that profession, then I realised that I was good at communicating in a relaxed way with different people. When my peers felt anxious on their placements about chatting to other professionals and the public, I had no anxiety at all!'*

Communication skills are important whether the communication is written in essays and reports or verbal in presentations and discussion with peers. Your ability to work as a team is important as you will be working with groups of other students where you will need to negotiate, delegate tasks and adapt according to the outcome of discussions. This will also include the non-verbal communication we use to support our verbal communication. Typically you will bring skills such as the ability to gather new information and make sense of it; writing reports, managing time and dealing with pressure. Finally you will bring to your studies some computer literacy. It is impossible to be an effective student if you are unable to word process, use journal databases or complete electronic searches on the internet. The university staff and others will contact you via email so it will be important to not only use these skills, but to do so in a professional manner.

Do I need to be practical or academic?

Occupational therapy will make a range of demands on you as a student and training is designed to be both academic and practical. This will be combined within the practice placement elements of the programme as you relate the theory learned at university to the practice setting. All students will be expected to demonstrate academic ability as the award of a final degree (or postgraduate qualification) is ultimately based on your ability to achieve satisfactory academic outcomes across the programme. These academic standards are strictly managed and will be rigorously applied through the assessment process and its related quality structures. You will be accepted on a programme because you have already evidenced the academic capacity to be successful, perhaps through your achievements at A level or their equivalents, an access course or a previous degree. Academic demands will be high but you will have the potential to succeed and will be supported by the university's academic team.

The practical element is slightly more ambiguous. Occupational therapy is often linked to a wide range of activities such as basketry or gardening, computing or cooking. While it is essential that you have a good understanding of these activities there is no expectation that you will be skilled in them. The occupational therapy course you undertake will give you opportunities to participate in similar activities and, more importantly, train you in understanding and appreciating the importance of them and their value as a treatment medium as these might be used as part of a treatment intervention in the same way as an occupational therapist might use dressing or preparing a meal.

Practice placements are a key focus for a student's practical skills. Here you will be given the opportunity to engage in a range of practical activities which will effect change in the clients you work with. The practical skills demanded of you will not require you to have prior expertise in this area but you may need to be able to replicate the skills of your educator. It is more important that you are observant and willing to take part. Further discussion of placements follows in Chapter 8.

Topics covered

Philosophy

Who you are as an occupational therapist is a concept which is explored early in your training. As an occupational therapist you will learn to view the world in a certain way. In establishing the occupational therapy worldview students will begin to appreciate why occupational therapists do what they do and how it makes a difference in people's lives. People are viewed as occupational beings. When we first meet someone in the street or at a party we usually end up describing ourselves by what we do – 'I'm Chris and I'm a lecturer (or husband, father, occupational therapist ...)'. In this way we define ourselves by what we do. The exploration of occupation can become an obsessive rite. Occupation becomes more than just the job. It becomes the place where I sit or work (I occupy space); it is the time consumed in the engagement; it is everything I do and say in a complete spatiotemporal context. This understanding of occupation will help you to identify the qualities unique to the occupational therapist. To some extent you will understand this because it may be this uniqueness which attracted you to the profession. The inclusion of the philosophy and professional perspective will offer an explanation of that uniqueness and provide you with the vocabulary to describe it.

This philosophy will also serve to explain the later aspects of the course. It will indicate the direction for future studies and direct the potential research possibilities of not only yourself but the profession as a whole. While there is no complete list of philosophical elements in occupational therapy the literature does indicate, amongst others, the importance of client-centredness, holism, occupation and of the need to enable clients. These qualities embody what occupational therapy is and while many will add their personal views to the list, the inclusion of these in occupational therapy practice will offer a better experience for the client group and greater satisfaction for the therapist. Understanding and embracing these views will help you to establish yourself as an occupational therapist. It is important as you consider a career in occupational therapy that you familiarise yourself with the professional paradigm and its spectrum of influence on practice.

The occupational therapy process

Like many other health professions, the occupational therapist will follow a predetermined routine when working with their client. This is known as the occupational therapy process. It has been considered at great length in academic literature because it is an essential aspect of therapeutic intervention. While there are many variations of this it can be considered to comprise four basic elements: assessment, planning, intervention and evaluation. As this is a cyclical process the final evaluation will serve as a new assessment. This is demonstrated in Figure 7.1.

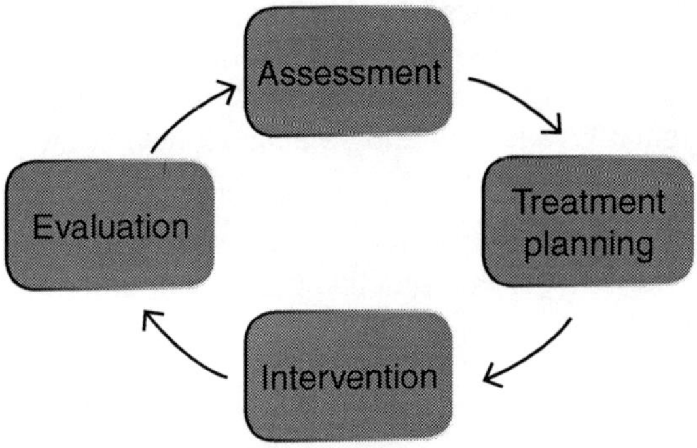

Figure 7.1: The occupational therapy process

The occupational therapy process is essential to occupational therapy practice and is applied in every practice context. The approaches and the language used may differ from place to place but the client experience will ultimately be the same with broadly the same outcomes. Whilst acute services may proceed quickly through the stages, other services may spend a long time focusing on an intervention which is drawn out.

Assessment is a process which draws together a range of information in order to establish what the needs of the client are, what resources might be available to the client and how these two factors might be brought together. You will be encouraged and enabled to develop your skills of observation, listening, insight and your ability to extract relevant data.

Once you have ascertained the level at which the client or service functions and have developed an understanding of their inherent functional difficulties, you will then be in a position to plan for their resolution or minimisation. Planning makes good use of the previously gathered data and taking into account the context of the intended intervention will help to resolve the situation. This must acknowledge elements such as motivation, culture, ethnicity and the personal needs and expectations of the client, their carers or the service. You will also begin to consider the importance of balancing this with the resources available to your team.

This plan needs to be implemented and early in your programme you will be given the opportunity to explore how you might interact with your clients and provide the intervention which you have developed. This may include practical skills on your part or the delegation of tasks to others.

When you have completed the intervention (or this part of it) it is appropriate to establish whether the plan and its implementation achieved the intended and desired outcomes. If this has been achieved the intervention was successful. If the goals have only been partially achieved or have wholly failed to achieve the desired outcome then it will be necessary to reassess and establish a new strategy for treatment.

The occupational therapy process will be observed, at least in part, when you experience your first practice placement and there will be an expectation that you are familiar with the process.

Practice placements

Early in your training as an occupational therapist you will have the opportunity to experience a practice placement. This will be discussed in detail in Chapter 8 but it is useful to realise that this experience will only be a snapshot of what occupational therapy is. While many students find placements stimulating and enjoyable, occasionally, students embarking on their studies become disillusioned in their first practice experience because they gain an alternative understanding of occupational therapy and this does not equate with their previous expectations. It is advisable to consider the role of the occupational therapist in a variety of situations before you commence training in order that you avoid this potential difficulty while also preparing you more effectively for application forms and interviews.

If this does happen to you, do not make snap decisions and withdraw from the programme. It is unlikely that you will have the same placement experience again and if this is an area you find particularly difficult then it is unlikely that you will take up future employment in this field. It is not necessary to enjoy all aspects of occupational therapy practice to be an occupational therapist – but you must be able to understand a wide range of therapeutic contexts and interventions. Your placement educators or university tutors will be happy to listen to your concerns and discuss them with you.

Your programme will offer a range of learning opportunities for you to prepare fully for placement. This will review elements such as placement documentation, teach you negotiation skills and train you in the practical skills of moving and handling. Learning these skills will allow you to fully exploit the learning potential of your practice placements.

Anatomy and physiology

Anatomy is the study of the human body and is of great importance to the occupational therapist. It considers the body structure and the relationship between body parts. We can understand more clearly how we undertake activities when we fully understand the way the body works. This may include surface anatomy where you will study the observable aspects of the body but you will also study the hidden components of the body such as the skeletal system or the nervous system. Physiology complements anatomy and is the study of the body as a whole, considering how the various elements of the body interact to function as a complete system. To some degree there is also a consideration of the effects of the environment on the human body. As these disciplines are so closely related they are generally taught together.

In your programme of study this may be taught as a discrete learning topic but may be combined with other subjects in order to offer a more integrated approach to your study. This might have a focus on the impact of disease or disability on the body or the manner in which the human body functions in response to certain stimuli or while completing certain tasks or activities.

This knowledge will be required in many clinical practice settings as supervisors or practice educators will use anatomical language with the expectation that you understand what they are saying. It is, therefore, advisable that you take a personal responsibility to ensure you have a good grounding in this subject. This is why the universities often request previous study of biological sciences at A Level or by other qualification. There will usually be an expectation that you are familiar with key terminology and that you are willing to learn.

Research

Throughout your life you have been exposed to research. If you have read the ingredients on a breakfast cereal box or looked at a bus timetable you have undertaken research and in your previous studies this will have been formalised in some way. Your training as an occupational therapist will advance your understanding of research. In the early part of your programme you will be exposed to research in a range of situations and you will learn about certain methodologies, how they work and where they will be most effectively used. Qualitative and quantitative methods will be explored and strategies for their application will be discussed. It is also likely that you will discuss the limitations of these research methods to avoid their use in inappropriate situations.

Research will be found in all your text books and make up the majority of articles in the journals which will underpin your assignments and learning. You will be directed to this research and expected to read it and understand it. This is an essential part of developing the skills for locating data and a practical teaching method to equip you with skills for study and for functioning as an occupational therapist. To exploit this it is advisable that you spend time talking with the staff in the library who are the real experts in finding this material and who will be happy to teach you. In the early stages of your training you will learn how to use evidence to substantiate your arguments and to introduce debate and critique to your work. In later years you will analyse and synthesise this material into your academic work and use this to validate your placement endeavours.

We all expect to have the very best care that is available and this can only be achieved when research is undertaken. Within healthcare this is presented through the notion of evidence-based and evidence-informed practice. In other words, we identify through research the very best strategies for intervention and then use this evidence to direct our practice as therapists. These are important concepts in healthcare and which will influence your studies and subsequent practice.

Getting the most out of lectures

Lectures are the educator's way of getting the most information to the greatest number of people. They are used to introduce a topic to a group of students but will not provide all the answers. A lecture can be seen as a way of transferring the ideas in a text book into something which is meaningful and relevant to the student. It will usually identify and bring to your attention the key ideas or debate relating to the subject matter, applying examples and explanations to the theoretical ideas of the topic. You will be signposted to influential thinkers in a topic and relevant texts and source material will be indicated.

As a student you should be thinking about how this information might be relevant to your previous study and the implications for practice. In order to make the most of this you should be preparing for every lecture. Where possible, many programmes will place copies of lecture materials on the university intranet pages, where these can be read beforehand or even downloaded and taken along to the session to support the presentation. This will help you to become familiar with the topic so that you can then focus on what is being said rather than copying the presentation. The notes you make are very important. Try to develop a note keeping system that will provide you with the best material. This is not about copying every word, but rather, it is about being selective in what you write. It may be necessary for you to develop your own abbreviations which would allow you to make notes more effectively, or perhaps you could use spider diagrams or mind maps to organise the material in a way which differs from just writing down every word. Some students try to avoid taking notes by recording the lecture. While this frees you up to listen more carefully, due to time constraints, students often do not listen to this material again. It is useful to view the recording as a backup only.

Case study: How to get the most out of lectures – Kara McLoughlin

'During my time at university I attended many lectures. Being in the lecture theatre isn't enough; I needed to fully participate to benefit. Spending that extra time preparing for a lecture or following up on notes after enabled me to keep up with my class and put me ahead when it came to putting theory into practice.

I needed to be prepared. It may seem obvious but printing and reading the PowerPoint presentation prior to the lecture helped me to have a basic grasp of the subject matter and generated my interest, which is an essential factor in becoming engaged. It also helped me to fully follow the flow of the lecture and I found I wasn't trying to write unnecessary notes as the information was already provided.

I found that following up and placing my notes in a well laid out folder meant that I could access them at a moment's notice. It was important to review my notes on a regular basis and read up on the issues I was unsure about. Getting ahead with my learning required effort and as an adult learner it was up to me to review the areas that had been covered in lectures.

When faced with the assignments I found that it was important to make myself familiar with the assignment criteria from day one. The subjects covered in the lectures prepared me for the assignments, giving me new knowledge and enabling me to reach my academic targets. You may not at first understand why there are particular lectures – but you should trust that the session is running because the experts have designed the programme. Use their expertise to support your learning. Don't be afraid to ask questions as others in the lecture theatre will probably be wondering the same things as you!

Although some of my tips might seem obvious, it is these short and simple tasks that tend to get put off. We blame time constraints and other commitments; however, I found that it was all worthwhile. I know that undertaking the programme takes dedication and hard work. Realise the wealth of knowledge readily available to you in lectures and seize the opportunity.'

When you have obtained your material from the lecture go back through it and try to organise your thoughts. You are likely to have forgotten most of the material discussed within a week so it is important that you make your material accessible. Highlight areas for additional consideration and use your study time to review this material and consolidate your knowledge.

Getting the most out of seminars

Seminars give students the opportunity to work on the practical aspects of the theory they have learnt. They are also a forum in which to develop discussion and presentation skills. Seminars usually involve the discussion of material presented in a lecture or in directed reading, exploring it in more detail than the lecture allows. You will be working in groups and often this will allow you to listen to and question the ideas shared by group members, giving you additional perspectives and insights into the subject material. It will also give you the opportunity to receive criticism and defend your own ideas. This may cause some anxiety and this is not uncommon. Many students do not like sharing their views openly or challenging other people's ideas. This can be embarrassing but can be managed. With thorough preparation you are more likely to be confident with the material you present.

You will get the most out of seminars if you prepare for them. Review the material you need for the seminar – you may have some directed reading or perhaps only the seminar title but you can use this to read around the subject. It will be useful if you have some ideas which you can introduce, or perhaps there are questions you need to have answered.

> *'I really enjoyed the seminars because it gave me a chance to ask questions and to learn in a practical way. We were in different groups each year, so I got to study with lots of different people.'*

As you participate in the session remember that you are there to learn as well as putting your ideas forward. Listening is an important skill and is very useful as you consider new subjects. Other people will offer alternative perspectives or will have read useful material that will increase your understanding of the subject so take notes on things being said. It is not just the tutor that will have something valuable to say; other students might also have some relevant comments and it is useful to write things down that are of interest. If there is something you do not understand ask about it and talk it through with the rest of the group. As others become involved in the discussions you have during these sessions you will develop your skills in group work and in presenting your material to others.

Sometimes the idea of speaking out in a group of people that you do not know well may cause anxiety but there are some strategies you can employ beforehand which will help you to deal with these feelings. Get to know the other group members, so that you feel more at ease. This will help the seminar feel like a discussion among friends. It may also be appropriate to challenge yourself to ask a question or make a contribution in each session to build your confidence. Participation does not require you to take over the session but to make a brief and relevant point or to respond to someone else's questions. Remember that seminars are there to help you learn not for you to show how much you know.

Getting the most out of tutorials

Tutorials move the focus for learning from the educator to the student. This can be quite intimidating for a student, at least in the beginning. Tutorials usually take place in small groups or perhaps as one to one sessions. They give students access to academic staff for focused teaching in particular subjects or support in managing their learning. In terms of learning the tutorial system can be very rewarding but it does make great demands on the student.

In traditional teaching the teacher is seen as the person who teaches and this is the role of lectures and seminars. The tutorial should allow you to use your tutor as a mentor who assists you in your development as a student and will aid you in more autonomous learning. Although you will have support from your tutor you need to recognise that you should be completing work independently outside of the timetabled sessions. The tutorial should give you the opportunity to review and critically discuss the material you have been considering both in the taught sessions and in your self-directed reading.

Top tips

- Prepare for tutorials by reading round the subject you will be discussing and by making a list of questions.
- If there is something in particular you don't understand or something you want the tutor to read, send the questions or reading material to the tutor before your tutorial. This helps them to prepare for you and stops you having to waste time while you watch your tutor read.

Other learning opportunities

University will offer other learning opportunities. This might include workshops or other practical sessions. These sessions will offer you the opportunity to try things out for yourself. Whether these are compulsory sessions in moving and handling, the control of infection, or perhaps the use of activities as treatment media, you will be learning how to actually complete the practical task. You will generally be facilitated through this process by a member of academic staff who will guide you through the procedure and offer suggestions on how to remember important details or techniques. You may have the opportunity to act as the client or the therapist in order that your colleagues can develop their skills. This will help you to begin to appreciate what a client may be experiencing if they were to participate in this task. It is often worth reflecting on these workshop experiences and using the opportunity as a springboard for additional learning.

Chapter summary

The first year of your programme will be exciting, tiring and fulfilling. As each week passes by you will learn more and feel increasingly able to piece information together to improve your understanding. There will be psychological highs and lows. Remember that all students experience this and that you are not alone. Take time at the end of the year to look back and reflect on everything you have learned. As well as refreshing your memory it will help you to celebrate how far you have progressed.

Key points

- At the beginning everyone will be new to the course – so you are all facing similar challenges.
- Plan for lectures, seminars and tutorials to ensure you are prepared.
- Read round the subjects to widen your knowledge and understanding.
- Be an active participant in your learning – don't just sit back and let others do the work.

Useful resources

Creek, J (2003) Occupational Therapy Defined as a Complex Intervention. *The British Journal of Occupational Therapy* 2012; 72(3): 10-115.

An interesting article and links relating to Kolb's experiential learning: Smith, MK (2001) 'David A. Kolb on experiential learning', *The Encyclopedia of Informal Education*. [Online] Available at: www.infed.org/biblio/b-explrn.htm [Accessed 1 June 2016].

Chapter 8

Occupational therapy practice placements

BPP UNIVERSITY SCHOOL OF HEALTH

Most students are eager to go out on their first practice placement and positive feedback about practice placements is very common on the end of course evaluations. So, what are placements all about?

What does being on practice placement mean?

A practice placement is the opportunity to try out in practice the theory you will have been learning in university. Each university programme will have different combinations of practice placement, with placements of different lengths, at different stages in the programme and with different marking criteria. When you are looking at which programmes to apply to, you should consider the practice placements as this may have an effect on your choice of programme.

When you start your training you will be told all about the practice placements at your university. All universities endeavour to provide students with a variety of placements in order to ensure every student has a broad range of experiences. The availability of placements depends on whether practice placement educators are available to take students. It is a complex task to allocate the right student to the right placement at the right time, and most universities will have a practice placement tutor who co-ordinates all of this. In order for you to be able to plan properly for your placement, you will be given advance notice of where you will be going and who will be your supervisor.

> *'Waiting to find out where I was going on my first placement was just like waiting for Christmas or my birthday when I was a child. I was sent to a palliative care team. I couldn't understand what sort of role an occupational therapist could have so when I contacted my educator I asked for some suggestions of books to read, which helped me to prepare.'*

It is your responsibility to contact the placement co-ordinator or supervisor in a timely way, to introduce yourself and to make any plans for your first day. You'll need to remember that if you don't write until the last minute or if you send only a cursory note, that this will be the first impression you give of yourself to the person who will be supervising and assessing your performance. Before going on practice placement you will need to have attended a substantial amount of theory lectures and seminars at university. All of your module work leading up to your placements is designed to give you the best theoretical knowledge in order that you can put this into practice. You will also have had the opportunity to think about practical issues, such as infection control, moving and handling, communication skills, lone working, consent and confidentiality. You should be given information regarding the kind of clothes to wear – whether this is your student uniform or smart casual clothes, information about jewellery, tattoos, body odour (yes, even that) and you should use this information to plan for your first day.

What activities will I undertake?

This will depend on the placement, your level of study and your level of competency. Each placement will have been graded so that you have the opportunity to develop your skills and reach higher goals on each subsequent placement. You will not be expected to know everything on your first placement – but by the end of year three there will be an expectation that you can work independently.

Some universities may have the first placement as an observation placement, where you are given the opportunity to shadow the occupational therapists to see what they do. Even on this placement you will be involved in carrying out some activities, for example writing up what you have seen and heard, attending case conferences, assisting with assessments.

Other universities may no longer have an observation placement and will expect you to participate in many more activities even on a first placement. Remember that when each programme is planned the academic staff will have thoroughly considered the information that they will need to teach you before going on placement in order for you to do this. This ensures that you are not dropped in from a great height without any sort of safety net!

> *'Although I feel I'm a reflective learner, I felt confident that my educator wouldn't ask me to do something that he didn't think I was capable of. This helped me to stretch myself and I was pleased with how much I was able to do.'*

You will be expected to undertake activities that fit with your level of training, both with and without supervision. Some students are reassured that their educator is with them when they try things for the first time and others feel better having a go before someone observes them – you should communicate with your educator to ensure they are aware of your preferred learning style. In order for your educator to make an informed decision about your competency, however, they will need to observe you undertaking the tasks at some point. This isn't to catch you out; it is to ensure you are safe.

There are lots of activities that you might be involved in, depending on the type of placement you are undertaking. At the very least, you will be assessing people's ability, communicating with many different people, planning interventions, carrying them out and evaluating their outcome. Some activities will by physical in nature (cooking, washing, dressing, football, painting), some will be psychological (anxiety management, concentration skills, relaxation training) and some will be social skills. The list is endless, so be open-minded and learn from everything that you have the opportunity to do. You will be expected to be enthusiastic, to seek out learning opportunities and to be forthcoming in your discussions about how and what you have been learning. Remember that you will need to demonstrate your learning to your supervisor, either by showing them or telling them.

Case study: Student experience of practice placement – Kate Smurthwaite

'My first four-week placement was a community and inpatient setting within a mental health service for older people. Prior to commencing my placement I arranged a pre-placement visit so that I would know where to go and what to do in an attempt to eliminate any first day nerves.

During the visit I was able to meet my educator, other occupational therapists and members of the multidisciplinary team. During the visit I was able to have a look around the wards and observe a pet therapy session with inpatient service users using two miniature horses, not at all what I had expected to see on this or any of my placements! The visit definitely helped to relieve any first day nerves.

Whilst on placement, I gained hands-on experience of the types of assessments, assessment tools and interventions used in this placement setting. This helped to put into context the theoretical knowledge I'd learnt at university but also meant I developed an understanding of things that were still to come during the course. I was also able to spend time with other professionals within the multi-disciplinary team to develop my understanding of their roles as part of the team.

My educator was very supportive of my learning, talking through contacts with service users, explaining her actions, asking my opinion and checking my understanding.

This placement allowed me to gain experience and develop my knowledge with a wide variety of physical and mental health conditions and what their impact can be on occupational performance.'

What hours will I work?

In total you need to complete 1,000 hours of practice placement, spread over the duration of your training programme. Each placement will be of a particular length and may have a small number of extra hours added to ensure that the placement is still viable if you are unable to go in for whatever reason. You will be expected to work full time during your practice placement, even if your supervisor is part time. Most universities allow for half a day personal study time in each week of placement and in most cases it will be up to you to negotiate this time with your supervisor. In the majority of cases, placements happen from Monday to Friday, however there are many services that are now operating seven days a week and you may be asked to work the same shift pattern as your supervisor, which may include some weekend work. Additionally, you may be allocated a residential placement, where you will be expected to stay overnight for some or all of the time. You will need to discuss your availability for these sorts of placements with the university practice placement tutor at the beginning of each new academic year, so that they are aware of your limitations.

Do I wear uniform?

Some practice placements will require you to wear occupational therapy student uniform. You will be informed by the university about the uniform requirements and how to order what you need. Hopefully, as long as you stay the same size for the whole of your programme, you will not need to buy any extra uniform! Many hospitals have a policy of having arms bare below the elbows (for hygiene reasons) and some hospitals are not keen to have staff with visible tattoos – so you may wish to check this out before making your application.

For health and safety reasons you will be asked to refrain from wearing jewellery – watches, badges, rings, piercings – as these can harm patients during moving and handling procedures or could be a danger for you if someone chose to pull on them.

Whether you wear uniform or not, you will need a sensible pair of shoes, as you will be surprised how much you will be on your feet during the working day. Health and safety suggests a proper shoe where your toes are covered.

If you do not need to wear a uniform on placement you will be expected to wear smart, casual, clean clothes. Men are advised not to wear a tie unless it is a clip-on tie, and again, the same points about jewellery and shoes should be noted. You need to remember that you are representing your profession so you need to look professional.

Although in the summer you might wish to be wearing a strappy T-shirt or sleeveless vest, the clients you are going out to see may not find it comfortable to see an expanse of cleavage or hot underarms! Likewise with trousers, you are strongly advised not to wear the modern style that sit across the hips. This is because when you bend over (which you undoubtedly will do) you will instantly reveal an expanse of your bottom that no self-respecting professional would want to show to their service user. Commonly referred to as 'builder's bottom', this can be avoided by wearing trousers that sit firmly around your waist.

Although it is unlikely that you will have to regularly wear your uniform at university, the same considerations about dress should be considered, especially if you are doing practical sessions.

Top tips

- If you have tattoos on your forearms check to see if this will cause a problem with uniform on placement.
- Review the clothes you have already to check you have a few suitable outfits to wear on placement.
- Invest in a comfortable pair of shoes for placement as you will spend lots of time on your feet.

Will I get support?

Support is normally offered to you in a number of ways while you are out on practice placement, depending on the university you attend.

You will be allocated a practice placement supervisor who you will work alongside and who will usually be your first port of call in any given situation. These supervisors will, in the majority, have completed an accreditation course in order to demonstrate their competence to educate students. The Accreditation of Practice Placement Educators (APPLE) scheme has been developed in order to give professional recognition to the role of the Practice Placement Educator and establish a nationally recognised scheme for the accreditation of practice placement educators that is transferable across regions.

They will have attended taught sessions at a university and have had their work assessed – on top of which they will have had experience working in their speciality as well as having educated students. They too have been student occupational therapists and understand the stresses and pressures that some students may feel on placement. They give their time to help students get the valuable experience they need to put theory into practice. You should be offered an opportunity to have some protected time with this person for your supervision each week – but most supervisors will make it clear that you don't have to wait until that session if you have a concern that you need to discuss.

Case study: Taking students on practice placement – Angela Bond

'I enjoy taking students on practice placements as I like to be challenged and questioned about my clinical practice. It is always a positive experience to clarify the reasons behind an assessment or intervention, seeing a situation through someone else's eyes.

There is a satisfaction in passing on knowledge and experience and possibly having an influence in the development of a student into an occupational therapist, directing them to the rewarding aspects of community work. I like to plan the placement so that the student experiences a wide variety of situations and conditions giving them a real insight into the reality of occupational therapy.

In university students learn the theory about models of practice, intervention and different conditions but all of this can be forgotten when faced with their first community visit. Supportive supervision should enable the student to overcome their initial anxiety of linking the theory to their skills in practice to develop their assessment, listening and liaison abilities.

During a placement I would expect a student to be able to carry out initial assessments, identifying needs and setting goals. They should also feel comfortable liaising with other members of the team, service users and their families. They should also have a clear understanding of the importance of following a person-centred approach and treating service users with dignity and respect.

My aim is that on successful completion of their placement the student should feel confident and positive about their experience, and will have learned a lot, both personally and professionally.'

There may also be a placement co-ordinator in the organisation that you are on placement in, who may be able to offer support. You will also be offered informal support from the other staff you will be working alongside. A member of academic staff from the university may also be allocated to you as the person who will either come out to visit you halfway through your placement or give you a phone call. This is a way to offer you support and to check that you feel you are getting the opportunities you need to learn. They can facilitate discussions between you and your placement educator, listen to your concerns and help you to decide how to move forward with any issues you feel you have. They will listen to the feedback your placement educator gives to you and will offer advice and suggestions where required. Some universities have a dedicated team purely for practice placement supervision, so you may be allocated to the same academic for all of your placements. Whatever the situation, you will have support from the university because your personal tutor is always contactable should you need to speak with them.

Some larger placement providers are able to set up student support groups if they have a group of students at the same time. There may be educational seminars, staff meetings or learning sets available for students to attend too.

All supervisors and academics will say that it is so much easier to support a student if the student is open and honest about any difficulties they may be having, whether it is at the placement or something happening outside that may be affecting their work. The sooner you enlighten someone about a problem the sooner it can be resolved, so you should never be worried about speaking to someone.

How will I be assessed?

Some universities base the placement assessment on a pass/fail basis, with the supervisor making this decision, while other universities ask the supervisor to give a numerical mark or a grade, linked to the university marking criteria. This information may help you to decide which university you wish to attend, as having a numerical mark or grade may make a difference to your degree classification at the end of your programme.

Whichever method is used, each programme will have an assessment form for the supervisor to fill in. You may be involved in this too. Some forms are written and some include a visual analogue scale, where progress is indicated on a continuum.

Unable to demonstrate the ability to reflect on the assessment process	____________	Able to demonstrate the ability to reflect on the assessment process
Comments:		

Figure 8.1: An example of a visual analogue scale

You will need to be able to demonstrate your competency against the criteria on the form. All of the criteria link to the Standards of Proficiency of the Health and Care Professions Council and the College of Occupational Therapists Professional Standards.

There is an expectation that you, along with your supervisor, will establish weekly objectives for the duration of the placement. Each week the objectives should enable you to demonstrate your learning towards the end goal of achieving the competencies. You will have the opportunity to discuss your progress each week in your supervision sessions. It is very important that you ensure that you have prepared for these sessions and that you take along all the evidence you need to support your claims of competency. If your supervisor has asked you to undertake a piece of work this should also be available for them to view. Equally important will be a reflection on your learning over the preceding time. This will help to show your educator how you have reviewed your opportunities, what you have learned from them and how you plan to develop.

If you are not achieving your objectives then your supervisor will point this out to you. They will give you examples of how you could improve and they will expect to see you put this into action. Remember that their feedback is given to you in order to help you to be as good as you can be and so you should try to accept this information with humility and a positive attitude. If you do not demonstrate an improvement or if your supervisor has a serious concern about your ability to practise, they will contact the university to discuss the options with your practice placement academic or personal tutor. It may be that they are able to agree an action plan over the telephone or the academic may feel it is more appropriate for them to come out to do an on-site visit. This is always meant in a supportive way, with everyone trying to help you to achieve the right level of competency. If you are not able to make the required changes, however, your supervisor may feel that you have failed to meet the competencies and your report will reflect this. Depending on your past record on practice placement, you may or may not be offered the opportunity to re-sit the placement, usually in a different service. Universities will only allow a student to fail two practice placements over the duration of a programme – if a student were to fail a third placement then this would result in them being asked to leave the programme. You will need to check the university policy on this before you decide which university to attend.

Professional suitability is a responsibility of all occupational therapists and student occupational therapists. It is a professional regulatory matter which is demonstrated by the adherence of each individual to the Code of Ethics and Professional Conduct for Occupational Therapists (2015) (herein referred to as the 'Code') published by the College of Occupational Therapists. This Code provides values and principles by which occupational therapists and student occupational therapists must abide for the protection of the public and to maintain high standards of professional behaviour at all times.

Students must be deemed to be professionally suitable to pass their placement and the Code can provide guidance for students and the supervisor throughout the placement and at formative and summative assessments. If a student had achieved all other learning outcomes, they cannot be deemed to have passed the placement unless the supervisor is satisfied that the Code has been adhered to with the student demonstrating and maintaining ethical and professional behaviour throughout their placement.

What about my safety?

Prior to your placement you will undertake any specialist training that your programme deems reasonable for your safety. Although you may have read or heard about incidents involving patients and staff, the number of incidents is extremely low and the majority of staff will have a long career without witnessing any incidents. What is most important is to recognise that if activities are planned, using up-to-date information and with reference to reducing risks then the likelihood of unsafe situation is minimised.

All placement establishments are required by the universities to be audited to ensure that they have the correct safety procedures in place. Fire, first aid, lone working and manual handling procedures are essential. Many universities will provide training in manual handling techniques for students as well as offering the opportunity for students to undertake conflict resolution training.

Where students are placed on placements in a secure setting, training will be provided by the placement to ensure students are aware of their responsibilities as well as the rules and safety precautions already in place. It is important to know that as a student you will be less likely to be left by yourself in any situation until your supervisor has had an opportunity to make an assessment about how you will cope. Harassment, whether verbal or physical, is not tolerated in any workplace, and there will be policies and support available for students. You should not be asked to undertake any task which is unsafe or which is beyond your competence.

While on placement you are covered by insurance, the detail of which will be explained by the placement team. You may need to increase your own car insurance if you will be expected to use your own car while on placement; however, a car is not a requirement of all placements and again, this will be something you will want to discuss with the university placement team or tutor.

What about 'non-traditional placements'?

A non-traditional placement is an exciting opportunity for occupational therapy students to undertake a placement where there is not normally a role defined for an occupational therapist. The way the placements are organised will depend on individual universities. It may be that you are allocated a placement or you may be given the opportunity to source your own placement.

Some non-traditional placements occur where there are no occupational therapists, with the idea that the student will use their clinical reasoning and research skills to demonstrate how an occupational therapist might be best used in the environment. This can be extremely exciting and there have been many success stories, where occupational therapy students have been so successful in demonstrating the benefits of employing an occupational therapist that the organisation has then moved forward and created a post. In these times of change in the National Health Service and social care, it is essential that occupational therapy students gain the skills to promote the profession as well as being able to create job opportunities for themselves.

Another form of non-traditional placement might be in a traditional setting, where the staff are interested in service improvement and ask the student to formulate how the service could be developed or altered to meet new needs. Again, the student will be using clinical reasoning and research skills to look at how the service could diversify or improve, with the resources at hand. The skills learned in this situation are extremely important, as change management and service improvement are a constant within any working environment.

Case study: Experience of a non-traditional placement – Richie Brown

'The non-traditional placement offered me the opportunity to combine the knowledge and skills I had learned from the first and second year theory and practice elements of the programme and put them into practice in a non-traditional setting. The experience I gained through university and practice placements gave me the confidence and skills to fully explain to the staff what occupational therapy had to offer. I was able to demonstrate how an occupational therapist would enhance their daily practice and the ideas I shared were really well received. This role allowed me to work autonomously, because I managed my own time and implemented my own ideas, conducting individual and group activities. I was given the opportunity to develop, implement and evaluate a person centred information gathering tool as the service did not already have one. This enabled me to use my research and development skills. I was accountable for the decisions I made and for ensuring that the tool I introduced was understood by the staff and the manager of the service. This new tool was then implemented and is currently being used collaboratively by the team and service users. As a result of this placement opportunity, the staff and managers felt an occupational therapist would be able to significantly contribute to their service, which has added to this rewarding experience. Through completion of the non-traditional placement I now feel ready to embark on an exciting and rewarding career as an occupational therapist.'

What is an elective placement?

An elective placement is a placement that a student arranges for themselves in an area of practice that is of interest to them. Some universities provide this opportunity to enable students to try a particular area of practice that might not normally be available regularly for students. It also gives a student the opportunity to work in an area of practice that they may eventually wish to work in. This will give them the chance to see if it is all they had imagined it to be. There may still need to be some negotiation with the placement team or tutor, to ensure the placement is suitable and that the practicalities such as insurance are covered.

Is there an opportunity to study overseas?

There may be an opportunity for you to undertake a placement overseas; indeed, many students take the opportunity to plan an elective placement abroad. Of course, this may take more planning on your part, but the students who the authors have known who undertook an overseas placement had nothing but praise for the experience. If you think this will be an important feature of the programme that you wish to apply for, then you should make sure you ask the admissions tutor about the possibilities and opportunities. If there is not a formal opportunity you may wish to arrange an overseas volunteering opportunity during your holiday.

Case study: Voluntary experience abroad – Harriet Penfold

'During the summer holidays of my second year on my BSc (Hons) Occupational Therapy programme I wanted to access extra practice experience to develop both my professional skills and to encounter a life experience that I would hopefully be able to transfer into my future career. I did so through searching on the internet for occupational therapy related volunteering opportunities. I came across a volunteering programme in Sri Lanka, specifically designed for occupational therapy. It was as simple as searching, filling in an application form and having a telephone interview. I explained my experience up to then and why I wanted the chance to be on the programme. The opportunity was incredible. Nine other student occupational therapists and myself spent five weeks learning about our profession from Sri Lankan professionals, and actually being able to implement what we knew under supervision. This increased my appreciation of providing client centred practice, as I was able to see how different the Sri Lankan culture is to my own, and why traditional theory and western practice is not always appropriate for all clients.'

Volunteering

Some universities may offer you the opportunity to undertake volunteering as part of the programme. Volunteering is an excellent opportunity to give something back to the community whilst learning about a charity and their work. Offering your time can be very rewarding – you may also learn new skills and add some valuable competencies to your curriculum vitae. The hours will not contribute to your practice placement requirements but may be a requirement of a module.

Chapter summary

Going on practice placement can be exciting and daunting at the same time. It is an opportunity for you to put into practice the theory you have been learning, and for many students who like to learn in a practical way, this is the opportunity to do just that. Getting to know your supervisor before you go on placement is an advantage, as it means you have one less person to introduce yourself to on your first day. Good planning is essential as well as having an open mind. Ask relevant questions at suitable times and make the most of every opportunity. After all, you may decide to apply for a post in the placement area after you graduate and you'll want the staff to remember you from your placement for all the right reasons!

Key points

- Plan for your placement by reading about the conditions you are likely to be treating.
- Contact the relevant practice staff early and in a professional manner.
- Follow the policies and procedures at all times.
- Don't be afraid to ask questions – your placement educator will expect you to do this.

Useful resources

The College of Occupational Therapists: www.cot.co.uk

Reference

College of Occupational Therapists (2015) *Code of Ethics and Professional Conduct for Occupational Therapists.* London: COT.

Chapter 9

What do the final years of studying occupational therapy involve?

BPP
UNIVERSITY
SCHOOL OF HEALTH

The final year of the programme will come around all too fast. In this chapter we will discuss how to plan for the final year and consider some of the opportunities and assessments that you might expect to encounter.

It will be tempting over the preceding summer holiday to make the most of the last long summer break you might have for a while; however, it is also a time that could be used to prepare yourself for the final modules. If you plan your time in advance you can have a balanced summer and return to your programme feeling refreshed and prepared. So, what are you preparing for? The final year is the opportunity for you to demonstrate how all of the theory you have so far learned about fits into contemporary practice. There will be a mixture of theory and placements and a final project or dissertation to complete.

As soon as you are notified of the timetable it is wise to plan your self-directed study time around this. Put time aside for each module and remember to check the dates that are published for the submission of assignments. Plan in any essential family or personal activities and time that you will rest. It might feel over organised; however planning ahead should reduce some of the stress later. The final year is not the year to attempt without preparation. Your degree classification will depend on the marks you receive in this year.

Is there a dissertation to write?

There will be different requirements regarding the final large assignment for each individual programme. In order to be awarded the 'Honours' element of any BSc programme a final dissertation or project must be undertaken and passed. The Honours element of the programme is essential for any student wishing to register with the Health and Care Professions Council as an occupational therapist – without this it is not possible to register and practise. Within MSc programmes a dissertation or research-based assignment will be required however many of these programmes allow students to opportunity to 'step off' at Postgraduate Diploma (PgDip) level, which would still allow them to practise as an occupational therapist.

A dissertation is the opportunity for students to demonstrate in one assignment the culmination of all their learning. There is preparation for the task through various research methods modules and no one is expected to automatically know how to complete the assignment. The dissertation may be primary or secondary research, carried out as individual students or in a small team and then written up as individual projects. Some programmes ask students to undertake a final project rather than a traditional dissertation. The size of the piece of work is similar but may be in the form of an extended research proposal, a business case or perhaps a service improvement plan.

With these large assignments, students are most usually allocated a supervisor from the academic staff team, who will support them throughout the activity. This supervisor will offer guidance, in line with university policies, on the academic element of the assignment as well as from a pastoral point of view. Some students do find this final assignment more of a challenge, mainly as it has been built up to be (through hearsay mainly) a difficult assignment to undertake. Academic staff will reassure students that the work is most certainly achievable if the student starts the work as soon as it is allocated, has a sound work plan and seeks support as soon as any issues arise. Many programmes offer a wide range of other methods of support, from comprehensive work books and module guides, access to research methods staff, e-learning resources and the opportunity to participate in group supervision. Group supervision has been shown to help to motivate students to get on with the work as they are prompted to do so by comparing their progress with that of their peers.

Case study: Writing a dissertation – Hannah Kay

'Writing a dissertation seems like an enormous feat: for me it definitely involved times where I questioned why I had even considered doing it in the first place. The whole experience is a combination of moments where it will feel like extremely hard work, breakthroughs that will energise you and keep you going and occasions where you may want to give up. Despite all this, though, writing a dissertation is something I would recommend. Although my dissertation was definitely a challenge, it was also one of the most worthwhile pieces of work I ever did. A dissertation provides the opportunity to consolidate all the things you've learnt over your course into something meaningful for yourself as you can explore your own ideas and interests. For me especially it was the chance to show what I was capable of and be creative as through a dissertation you can investigate new or alternative areas of practice that may not have been covered in your modules. This also makes it an excellent opportunity for personal and professional development because you have the space to explore your passion and consider it within a wider context, creating greater understanding which may also be usefully applied in your future career. Through the process you also develop useful skills such as how to be concise, communicate ideas effectively and manage your own time. The end result is a proper piece of academic work to be proud of that definitely makes it worth all the effort.'

These comprehensive assignments may have additional elements to them as well as having a large expected word count. Most Master's level dissertations will also involve a *viva voce*, where the work is presented to a small panel who will ask questions about the various elements of the work. Some final projects will involve this too. Often there is a requirement to produce a poster or electronic poster around which the presentation will take place. The panel will usually comprise at least one academic staff member plus one or more of the following people: practice staff, service users, students or external examiners.

> *'This may sound strange, but I really enjoyed presenting my dissertation. It felt like all of my hard work was being admired and because I knew my topic in so much depth, it was easy to answer any questions!'*

This is the student's opportunity to demonstrate their knowledge of the subject they have just spent months studying and should help to give them the confidence to go on to submit their work to their peers at a conference or other proceedings. Many students do this and it is a joy to listen to the findings of their work.

Will there be option modules?

Some programmes may offer final year students the opportunity to study a particular area of practice in more depth via an optional module. Where this is available students can develop their skills in a particular area of practice or management. Option modules may also be offered at other times in the programme but tend to be scheduled later on as they are usually building on the core material that has been delivered earlier in the programme. It is useful to know that even mandatory modules in a final year are often more flexible in the way work is undertaken. In many cases the assignment brief entails the student choosing an essay title, selecting an area to undertake an elective or role emerging placement and deciding on a topic for their dissertation or final project. In this way, students are given the opportunity to develop areas of interest. It is useful to discuss your ideas with your personal tutor to ensure that you are not choosing topics that are too similar. It would not be sensible to undertake all your third year assignments around one condition or client group as this may lead you to have too narrow a learning experience.

In addition to this, some programmes offer students the opportunity to participate in an Erasmus+ exchange. This is where students are able to study abroad in a partner university or practice placement. Each programme has different opportunities available to students. If the opportunity to study abroad is one of the key requirements on your list then you should remember to check the up-to-date details of each available educational programme on the College of Occupational Therapists website and then contact the admissions tutor to confirm that these opportunities are still available.

Finally, some programmes offer students the opportunity to undertake additional training free of charge. It might feel like this could put extra pressure on the final year student; however it is certainly worth considering all the opportunities available. Some examples of additional training worth consideration are the European Computer Driving Licence (ECDL) or a British Sign Language (BSL) qualification. Most universities also provide free or low cost summer school places for existing students, so it is worthwhile looking at these opportunities too. Look out for courses that other schools or faculties are running as well as the health and social care opportunities. You may find that the Business School or faculty within the university can offer useful short courses on business planning, accounting and other useful skills for the individual who may be keen to set up in independent practice. Another useful contact will be the Enterprise department, who will be able to advise you on extra support if you have a new business solution or an idea for a new piece of technology or equipment that you would like to develop.

Preparing for practice

The final year of study offers the opportunity to develop the additional skills required for the competent practitioner. Up to this point there will have been a great number of skills to learn that have been directly linked to practice with service users. There is a raft of other professional skills that students will be given the opportunity to develop ready to transition from being a student to being an independent practitioner.

Many final year students contemplate how different it will be to have to take full responsibility for their actions when they qualify. This is because even though there has been a steady progression during practice placements from being a novice to becoming competent in the final placement objectives, there will have always been a practice educator or supervisor around to check each unknown with. Some students express a view that as students they didn't feel it was their place to challenge other staff when something didn't seem quite right because they were 'just a student'. The realisation that this will not be an acceptable reason for non-action looms heavy and some students feel concerned about whether they will be assertive when the situation calls for it. In addition to this, students need to be able to begin to trust in their own intuition and reasoning skills in order to build their self-confidence. This should be facilitated through the practice placement element of the programme as well as through the final year assignments but there will be other opportunities for the proactive student to test themselves out before they complete the programme.

At the beginning of the final year it is essential to reflect upon the skills already learned and those that are yet to be addressed. Carrying out a simple strengths, weakness, opportunities and challenges (SWOC) analysis and then linking this to a learning contract should help to add some structure to your self-development. A learning contract is a formal document you might develop with your tutor, which will identify areas for development and learning. It should include areas for development, resources to be used and a timescale for completion. By this time in your training you will have developed the ability to look widely for learning opportunities, so the learning contract will be an in-depth document that guides you towards a variety of ways to validate your learning. It is certainly a document that you can use when meeting with your personal tutor to discuss your progress.

Getting peer support from the student forums hosted by the College of Occupational Therapists may be another area that you could investigate. The networking opportunities are invaluable and there are often student conferences and study days available at low cost. If your own university has a student group then this is certainly something you should be actively involved in during your final year, as there may be opportunities that come along that would enhance your skills.

Developing a continuous professional development (CPD) portfolio

A CPD portfolio is a file of evidence that you will need to demonstrate your competency. You may be asked by the Health and Care Professions Council to provide this file of evidence at the biennial renewal of your registration; this means your registration and therefore your ability to practise and earn your living will be dependent on the evidence you are able to provide. It is surprising how many students leave the development of a CPD portfolio until the last minute and then realise that it would have been so much better to start it at the beginning of the programme, as the tutors had suggested! You will need this portfolio for the whole of your career, so it is sensible to create a portfolio that is easy to maintain and access.

There are CPD portfolio templates available from a number of sources; your university is likely to provide you with a template or you could access a template from the College of Occupational Therapists. If you decide to make your own template, then there are structures you could follow. As an example you may like to use the National Health Service Knowledge and Skills Framework (Department of Health, 2004). Every occupational therapist has to be able to meet all core dimensions at level 2 and be able to meet the health and wellbeing (HWB) dimensions (HWB6 and HWB7) at level three. You will need to develop a way to cross reference your evidence, as some evidence will satisfy more than one competency. Whether you do this with letters, numbers or colours is up to you, as long as it is clear and presented in a professional way. Further details on the Knowledge and Skills Framework can be found in Chapter 10.

The evidence you provide to demonstrate your competency should be relevant, contemporaneous and not breach confidentiality. You will need to provide a series of evidence and be able to show that the demonstration of the skill was not just a one-off stroke of luck. So, if you have attended a study day and have been given a certificate that would make a good start, but shouldn't be used as a stand-alone piece of evidence. With it should be the rationale for attending the study day, a reflection on the things that have been learned and an action plan to show how you intend using the skills in practice. Then to follow this up, a reflection after you have been using the skills for a while, to show how you have progressed would also add weight to the evidence. You may seek testimonies from peers to supplement your evidence; however, it is useful to ensure the facts are specific rather than a general statement about how nice you are! It is unnecessary to seek to use testimonies from your service users as this could breach their confidentiality. There are so many other effective ways to demonstrate your competency that will not put you at risk of breaking your Professional Code of Conduct.

Top tip

It is not necessary to keep a hard copy (paper based file) of your evidence. Keeping all your information secure on a computer – remembering to keep a backup of this on a disk or memory stick – will make it easier to keep the information up to date and tidy. In this way, when you want to create a CPD file of evidence for an interview for example, you can print off specific, crisp, clean documents and put them into a professional file for the occasion. For the hoarders this method also means that you rarely need to actually throw anything out as you can move out of date evidence into a separate file once it is no longer of use.

Final exams

Many programmes have moved away from 'finals', the dreaded final exams at the end of a three-year programme. Within a Master's level programme there may be a formal exam in the form of a *viva voce* element of the dissertation. It is certainly worth checking with individual admissions tutors to clarify this. In order to elicit depth of knowledge at the final stages of training any exam would be likely to be a written piece rather than multiple choice. Some exams are 'seen' in that the student is told the question or choice of questions before the exam in order to prepare. Needless to say, the well prepared student has nothing to fear.

The National Student Survey and the Postgraduate Taught Experience Survey

During your final year you will be invited to participate in the National Student Survey (NSS) if you have undertaken a BSc (Honours) degree or the Postgraduate Taught Experience Survey if you have undertaken a PG Diploma or Master's level degree. This is your opportunity to feedback about the whole of the programme you have undertaken. You may have used the results of this feedback from previous students to help to make your application choices and so future students may well value your thoughts and opinions to help them make theirs.

Remember to give feedback about the whole programme, not just the stressful bits. It is essential that you try to keep your emotions from colouring your judgement – try to assess things objectively before submitting something that you regret later. Remember that it is not only students who read the survey, employers do too. If they read negative things about a particular training programme it may put them off employing someone from there. You will have many opportunities to give constructive feedback to your programme team throughout your time on the programme. You will be told how this feedback has been used and why changes are made so you should feel reassured that the team are taking your feedback very seriously.

As the final year progresses you will be able to assess your progress through the marks and feedback you have been given. Don't go it alone or feel you should know all the answers; your personal tutor, the module teams and the programme leader will all still be happy to help you if you are having a difficult time. They understand that students are all different and have different threshold levels to stress – after all, they have all undertaken the occupational therapy training themselves as well as other postgraduate training at Master's and Doctorate level.

Enjoy the opportunities, share your knowledge with other students and celebrate when the final assessment is submitted. It is not the end of the learning process as you will be continuing your professional development throughout your career, but it should be the last formal assignment you have to undertake for a little while at least!

Chapter summary

It is surprising just how quickly the final year of your programme will go. Think carefully about the topics for any assignments where you have a choice. You may be able to tailor an assignment to target a key contemporary issue, which may be useful to you later when you are applying for jobs. The final year is an opportunity for you to show how much you have learned and your assignment marks will define your final degree classification – so aim high!

Key points

- Plan your study and relaxation time before you start your final year – and try to stick to it.
- Dissertations or final projects are only hard if you start working on them too late and fail to take advantage of the support offered.
- Don't narrow your skills and experiences in the final year to areas you are interested in at that time. In the future you may need a wider knowledge base.
- Start your CPD file early to reduce unnecessary stress later.
- Don't be afraid of seeking help and support.

Useful resources

OT programmes in the UK: www.cot.co.uk/become-ot/ot-programmes-uk

Reference

Agenda for Change Project Team (2004) *The NHS Knowledge and Skills Framework and the Development Review Process.* London: Department of Health.

Chapter 10

What career paths are available to me?

BPP UNIVERSITY SCHOOL OF HEALTH

In this chapter we will consider the career paths available to the graduate occupational therapist. Additional information that is crucial to inform your choice of career, such as insurance, mentorship and being part of a professional community are also discussed. It is never too early to start thinking about the kind of role you would like to have. Try not to limit yourself too early in your training though, or you may find that you miss out on opportunities. As the contemporary landscape of employment changes, you will need to consider all of the options open to you. The job you want may not be on your doorstep and you may need to revise your plans if you are unable to move readily. Keeping an open mind and being prepared to try different options will make you more flexible within the employment market. First of all we will consider how to get your first job.

Getting your first job

During your final year you will start to think about what you intend to do at the end of your time as a student. All universities have careers advisers who can help you with application forms and practice interviews. Some programmes will offer students the opportunity to undertake practice interviews as part of the programme itself and some may have dedicated careers staff assigned to them, which is useful as they should have experience with occupational therapy applications to draw upon.

> *'I was mortified when I realised I was going to have a practice interview! I was so anxious and knew I was wriggling in my seat. After the practice our group sat together and gave each other feedback. I was surprised that people thought some of my answers were good. I used the feedback to help me prepare for the real interview and I was offered the job!'*

It may come as a surprise to learn that not all graduates choose to go into occupational therapy straight away. Some will take a gap year to travel and work abroad. Remember that if the programme you have studied was accredited by the College of Occupational Therapists then you will also be able to work in any countries that are part of the World Federation of Occupational Therapists.

You may wish to find a post in a traditional setting, such as the National Health Service or social services. Nearly all jobs in these areas are now advertised electronically on sites like Sector 1 and NHS Jobs. You will need to register with these organisations and then, after indicating the types of job, location and pay band, you will get a notification whenever a job is advertised that meets your requirements.

Other places where you will find jobs advertised are the *British Journal of Occupational Therapy* (*BJOT*) and *OT News*. Both of these publications are available to members of the College of Occupational Therapists as part of the subscription. *BJOT* may be available in the university library too. Here you may find some highly specialised posts and often advertisements for the different employment agencies that offer locum work.

Locum work may appeal to you, especially if you do not have any dependents or commitments. Locum postings can last from a few days to several months – even years if a post is difficult to fill. You will need to have a degree of flexibility and feel very comfortable in new situations. This kind of work as a first post can be daunting, as you will be expected to function without a huge amount of supervision.

Some private healthcare organisations also employ occupational therapists, especially in their special needs units. This can be a challenging area to work in and you may need to arrange your own supervision externally.

You may wish to work in a non-traditional setting – perhaps a charity or school. Many charities advertise posts locally as well as on their websites, so keep checking in the local press for posts. The *Times Educational Supplement* (*TES*) is a useful first point of call for jobs in education (both Local Authority and independent schools). You might have had the opportunity to undertake a role emerging placement in a non-traditional setting and may decide to approach the organisation for a post there, especially if you made a good impression!

There are also now increasing roles for occupational therapists in residential and nursing homes. A significant amount of rehabilitation occurs in these settings and the work can be extremely satisfying. Check the Care Quality Commission (CQC) site for up-to-date information about any residential or nursing home, as the CQC regularly inspects organisations and can give an objective view. Indeed, you may decide to work for the CQC as either an inspector or a specialist adviser.

For any job that you apply for you will need to put time aside to complete the application form. All jobs will ask for a personal statement of some sort and it is important to get this right. As so many new graduates will fit the qualifications of the post, it is important you demonstrate that you are the best person for the job through the information on your application form. Take time to read the person specification and respond to the attributes required, indicating how you meet the criteria. Try not to say 'I can do this' or 'I'm good at that' as it really doesn't demonstrate your skills. Give an example of how you meet the criteria to show your competency. The quality of your application form will be the thing that gets you through to an interview. This is then your opportunity to show a panel why they should select you. Again, you should take time to plan for the interview, think about how you might answer the questions and prepare a file of evidence to take with you.

Starting your own business

Starting your own business is also a possibility but requires a lot of enthusiasm and experience as an occupational therapist, as there is less easily accessible, daily professional support. Some business experience would also be very beneficial. This might be your own experience or from a support organisation. There are many independent practitioners working for themselves and undertaking private work. This work may be in a specific field, for example insurance work or paediatric assessments and treatment. Most universities have a business unit or entrepreneur centre where business advice can be sought and of course, there is a special interest group at the College of Occupational Therapists for occupational therapists in independent practice. You will need to identify the gap in the market and prepare a business case so you can approach a lender for the set-up costs. There are many issues to consider: insurance, work base, security, supervision, marketing and sustainability to name a few. Whether you intend offering peripatetic sessions to a school or offering full-time cover to a nursing home, there are risk factors to balance with the pleasure of determining your own career path. Some of the following information in this chapter will be very important for you to note.

Registering with the Health and Care Professions Council (HCPC)

If you intend practising as an occupational therapist you will need to apply to register with the Health and Care Professions Council (HCPC). The HCPC is the regulatory body for occupational therapists. As a regulatory body, the HCPC protects the public by keeping a register of all occupational therapist who meet the HCPC standards for training, professional skills, behaviour and health. 'Occupational therapist' is a professional title protected by law. Individuals who are not registered with the HCPC are not allowed to use this title and to do so is classed as a criminal offence. Occupational therapists are required to re-register bi-annually and may be asked to provide evidence of their continuous professional development in order to fulfil this. If you fail to meet the standards you may be removed from the register, which would mean that you would no longer be able to use the professional title or work as an occupational therapist. It is very important to remember to re-register because if you do not, even if you meet the standards, you may be temporarily unregistered and an employer may suspend you (possibly unpaid) until you are back on the register. This is a costly waste of time and to be avoided.

Top tip

To apply to register you will need to download the application forms from the website, collect the evidence required and get your forms signed by the appropriate people before sending them off with a cheque for the fees. Some employers will not consider your application if you have not already registered, so it is wise to apply as soon as your programme completes so that the forms are waiting at the HCPC ready to be dealt with as soon as your university advises them that you have been successful.

Joining your professional body

The British Association of Occupational Therapists (BAOT) is the professional body for occupational therapists in the United Kingdom. This body acts as a trade union, lobbying on your behalf and influencing the direction of the profession in a wide variety of organisations. The College of Occupational Therapists (COT) is a subsidiary of the BAOT. It is the College of Occupational Therapists that sets the standards of education and the professional standards. The College of Occupational Therapists provides a wide range of resources for students and professionals, some of which have been discussed in previous chapters of this book.

Students are encouraged to join the BAOT as a student member from the beginning of their programme. Some universities will pay for this while others may not. (See also Chapter 6, section *Are there professional costs related to my course?*) The range of support and learning materials available via the website are ever growing and are invaluable throughout training. As well as this information, the College of Occupational Therapists holds an annual conference where the professional community gets together to share innovations, research and experiences as part of a shared learning event. It is an opportunity to meet with the researchers and practitioners who are leading the way in occupational therapy practice. As you come to the end of your training programme you will need to consider transferring your membership from that of student member to full professional member.

There are many benefits to being a member of the professional body, all of which are available in their literature and on the website. Just paying your subscription to be a member of the professional body is not enough evidence to demonstrate you are keeping up to date, although it is a start. The organisation itself is member led, which means that it relies upon its members to fully engage in its activities. This could be in the form of joining a local or regional group, attending study events, volunteering to become a BAOT steward, joining and participating in a specialist section or putting yourself forward to become a member of Council. You could be Chairman of Council in the future – it is a role open to any upstanding member of the professional community.

It may also be fruitful to join the World Federation of Occupational Therapists (WFOT). A member of WFOT can gain insight into the internationality of occupational therapy. The scope of professional practice, from country to country differs tremendously and WFOT supports relationships between countries, individual practitioners, educators and students. WFOT also has practical relationships with a large number of international organisations. It works closely with the World Health Organisation at both a central and regional level.

Professional indemnity

Professional indemnity insurance is provided through membership of the BAOT. This indemnity cover is for claims made against you in the United Kingdom and covers negligence, omission and error. At present the indemnity insurance cover is for up to £5 million (excluding people working in private practice, who will need to obtain further insurance if their fee income is more than £1,500 per annum (COT, 2014)). If you work within a statutory organisation you will automatically be covered by their insurance too. For all other kinds of employment it is advisable that you ask about the insurance arrangements and seek professional advice to ensure that you have the right level of cover. This is where being a part of the professional body is invaluable, as this advice can be sought from BAOT at no cost.

Preceptorship and mentorship

Starting your first job can be stressful, whether you are in a large and busy department or working independently. Many organisations now offer a system of preceptorship for new graduates to help to support them through the first six months of their new role. Each organisation will have different guidelines, but the principles are similar. It you would like to look at an example of a preceptorship programme then the College of Occupational Therapists has a very useful and comprehensive preceptorship handbook that is available for members to download.

Mentorship is when you select someone to support you through a period of your career. It is unlikely to be your employer or line manager; rather it should be someone with relevant experience who is at a distance from your working environment. Their role is to facilitate your thinking and decision-making by asking you sensible and relevant questions to help you to work out the best course of action. They should give you honest feedback. A mentor who always agrees with everything you say is not being truthful to the process. Equally, a mentor who only points out the negatives could seriously undermine your confidence. It is important to establish some ground rules with your mentor. Decide how long this relationship will last and the specific goals you wish to achieve. Take time to evaluate the process so you keep on track. You should choose a different mentor for the different situations you encounter and want to develop in, to ensure you have the right person supporting you.

The NHS Knowledge and Skills Framework (KSF)

The NHS KSF (Department of Health, 2004) was developed to provide a specific framework of the knowledge and skills required by all of the different staff (except dentists and doctors) who work within the NHS. It defines and describes the skills in a consistent way and it will be used (if you work in the NHS) to review your development and progress. It should support the direction of your continuous professional development (CPD) and can be used to form the framework for your CPD file of competencies.

It is wise to take time to understand the framework as it is a very useful structure to help describe the acquisition and development of your knowledge and skills. You show how you use your knowledge in practice, how you have developed to be able to undertake more complex interventions and how you have put your postgraduate training into practice. It is very important that you are able to show that you are keeping your skills up to date. Quality services depend on the staff within them maintaining their competencies – after all, you wouldn't want to be treated by someone who hadn't bothered to keep up to date.

Whether you work in the NHS or not, this is a very useful tool. You can download a copy from the Department of Health website.

Choosing a speciality

Many students arrive at the occupational therapy programme with an idea of which area they would like to work in when they eventually qualify. Others may have been seconded by their employer to undertake their training. If this is the case for you, you may be returning to a particular area of work and may need to fulfil a contractual obligation before making your first career choices. One thing is for sure, during the programme you will have been given the opportunity to experience occupational therapy in a number of practice placement settings and also through theoretical study within the university. Your ideas may have changed and you will need to evaluate the kind of jobs you will be looking for.

One opportunity that may be available to you is a rotational post. A rotational post is when an employer offers a job that allows you to work in several different occupational therapy services in turn. Each rotation can usually last from between four to six months. Some rotations are 'mixed', where you are able to rotate through both physical and mental health departments, others are limited to either all physical or all mental health. Some services are able to offer mixed rotations that are in the NHS and social care – there are many different possibilities. A rotational post allows you to try different areas of practice before deciding the area you want to specialise in.

Specialising doesn't happen straight away. You can expect to be in a graduate post for up to two years in order to begin to feel really confident in your skills. It is advisable not to move up the professional grades too quickly, as this tends to prevent you from really learning the competencies to gain a solid base from which to practise.

Becoming a consultant occupational therapist

There are opportunities for occupational therapists who become specialised in a particular area to apply for a consultant post. These posts were developed to enable practitioners to have a senior clinical and leadership role. As well as delivering expert clinical practice, you will be expected to undertake some teaching in this role and would certainly be expected to undertake research audit and the evaluation of treatment and services. It is a great opportunity to be a key leader and influencer in strategic and service changes. Your research will create the evidence base that will improve services.

Taking the management path

Becoming a manager is a rewarding and challenging role. There are management roles within large and small teams, and you may feel that you have the skills to manage a service in an efficient and effective way. You will need to have developed excellent leadership skills in order to undertake these management roles well. If you enjoy personnel management, budgeting, planning and evaluation then this is the challenge for you. You may find yourself managing your own business or managing a diverse team within one of the statutory services. Being a leader in this way isn't for everyone and can divert you away from working directly with service users, but the opportunity to ensure services are as good as they can be is equally satisfying. A role in management is often taken following additional postgraduate studies in leadership or management and these will help you develop your skills and enhance your understanding of the theories and practicalities of leadership.

Case study: Becoming a manager – Judith Metcalfe

'Management had not been in my career plan; however, when offered the chance of an eight-month secondment into an operational managers post, albeit management of a small occupational therapy department, I thought why not – a chance to learn new skills, try something different, and hopefully develop a wider understanding of the workings of the NHS – all without risk to my substantive post; so an opportunity not to be missed. I enjoyed the eight months, found it quite difficult to go back to my day job, and eventually ended up with the post permanently.

Despite it not being in my career plan, I found I had naturally tended towards CPD with a management slant – Recruitment and Selection, Dealing with Difficult People, and Leading an Empowered Organisation to name a few training examples. Without these, it would have been more difficult. I had also been encouraged and supported in volunteering for relevant projects. The permanent post gave me an opportunity for further CPD – after a significant gap without formal academic work, I found myself completing a Master's. This certainly increased my awareness of the NHS and some of the challenges it faces.

Management is not an easy option, but it does offer the chance to influence and develop services that you care about within the ever-changing environment of the NHS. These are challenging times in the NHS – learning to see some of the challenges as opportunity is beneficial. Although there is the risk that you move further away from clinical involvement, being a manager still allows you to support clinical staff in their development – watching a new band 5 learn and grow in ability and confidence is still something that gives me a lot of satisfaction.'

Becoming a researcher

During your training you will have ample opportunity to read and discuss other people's research. Creating the research evidence on which best practice is based is an essential role within the profession. If you are able to attend the National Conference you will be able to listen to presentations about the research that has been carried out – it is an inspirational experience! Depending on the programme you study, you may have the opportunity to undertake your own small scale research, be involved in others' research or develop an extended research proposal. You will understand the types of research that can be undertaken, how to interpret the outcomes and how to use this to shape the interventions you use every day in your practice.

It is essential that all occupational therapists contribute in some way towards creating the body of evidence required for the profession. You may decide to look for a research post, usually based in a university research department or teaching hospital. Here you will get the opportunity to undertake your own research and get paid to do so. Another way to undertake research is via further academic study – moving on to a Master's level programme and a Doctorate (PhD). Usually you undertake these kinds of study at the same time as working – which has its positive and negative aspects. Some PhD students are full-time students who are paid. Again, there are a wide range of ways to undertake further study, so you should look around to see what suits you best.

Thinking about teaching

All occupational therapists need to be trained and teaching is another way to help to share your skills in order to help others achieve their goals. As a practitioner you should get the opportunity to participate in students' practice placements – either for one-off activities or as their placement educator. As a specialist you may be invited to give special lectures within the occupational therapy programme too. Once you have had the chance to try out your teaching skills you may consider a teaching post. Most lecturer posts require you to have studied a Master's degree. Some universities will sponsor you to undertake a Master's as part of the conditions of your employment. You will also need to undertake and pass a Postgraduate Certificate in Learning and Teaching in Higher Education (PGCLTHE), or similar.

Case study: Becoming a lecturer – Nina Bedding

'I have loved my career so far as an occupational therapist and found great job satisfaction from patients, colleagues and students that I have had the privilege of working with. Over 15 successful years in the acute physical setting initially in a clinical role and then as a Service Lead I have worked with many graduate staff and students to develop them personally and professionally while tackling some particularly challenging situations that arise in the NHS today. Working with students and watching them develop and share the enthusiasm that I have for occupational therapy has always given me a great sense of joy and accomplishment.

As my role as Service Lead developed beyond occupational therapy it forced me to reflect upon my career. I realised that my next step had to be into the area which I found fulfilling. The opportunity to become a lecturer arose and the idea of being able to share 'real life' experiences and knowledge to enable others to learn was appealing. Being able to work with students on a daily basis to shape the future workforce of occupational therapy really excited me.

Nine months into my role as a lecturer, I am loving it. I really enjoy working with the students while still maintaining my links with clinical practice. Although I have not yet completed a full academic year and I still feel very new to the role, I am enjoying the variety of work and the challenges that the students bring. I am excited for what the future holds as a lecturer.'

Working internationally

The occupational therapy qualification (if this has been undertaken via a College of Occupational Therapists accredited programme) is recognised in the countries that belong to the WFOT.

If you plan to work in the USA you will need to start the application process almost as soon as you start your final year. To work in the USA you will need a Master's degree, so if you have studied a BSc (Hons) programme you will need to complete a fast track Master's programme before you can apply. You will be able to find out which universities offer this kind of programme from the College of Occupational Therapists website. There are plenty of overseas recruitment agencies that will be looking to sign you up. They each offer different packages, so it is worthwhile attending their publicity days to find out more before you sign any contracts. Some countries will require you to undertake additional examinations in order to register to work there. Going through an agency will make it easier to find this out, however you can contact the specific Health Board for the country you would like to work in to get the up-to-date information you need.

If you are planning to work in the Republic of Ireland there is a complex application process to undertake. Your personal tutor and placement tutor will need to provide a variety of evidence too, so it is advisable to discuss your application with them before you complete your final year. Further information on international perspectives is included in Chapter 13.

Chapter summary

As an occupational therapist there are so many opportunities available to you that you may have difficulty deciding on your career path! While some people will concentrate on getting a job and making short-term plans, others may have a long-term career pathway in mind that requires careful planning. Whatever you plan to do, make sure you keep your programme leader or personal tutor informed when you get your first job, as this is important information they will need. Your tutors will be interested to hear about your progress over the years too and you may find yourself being asked back to share your experiences.

Key points

- Submit your application for the Health and Care Professions Council register as soon as you complete your programme and remember to re-register every two years.
- Discuss your employment plans with your personal tutor – they may be responsible for writing your reference so they need to know all about you.
- Plan your future direction of study so that you have the correct level of degree for the career of your choice.
- Join your professional body and be an active member – this will offer you support and enhance your continuous professional development.

Useful resources

Sector 1: http://sector1.net/

NHS Jobs: www.jobs.nhs.uk/

College of Occupational Therapists (2006) *The preceptorship training manual: a resource for occupational therapists.* London: COT.

The Department of Health: www.dh.gov.uk

The World Federation of Occupational Therapists: www.wfot.org

Council of Occupational Therapists for the European Countries: www.cotec-europe.org

The American Occupational Therapy Association inc: www.aota.org

Occupational Therapy Australia Ltd: www.otaus.com.au/

References

Agenda for Change Project Team (2004) *The NHS Knowledge and Skills Framework and the Development Review Process.* London: Department of Health.

BAOT (2012) *BAOT Malpractice and Public Liability Insurance.* [Online] Available at: www.cot.co.uk/sites/default/files/corporate_documents/public/insurance-summary2012.pdf [Accessed 27 May 2016].

Chapter 11

Occupational therapy in the statutory sector

BPP UNIVERSITY SCHOOL OF HEALTH

In this chapter we will consider the work undertaken by occupational therapists who work within the National Health Service (NHS) and the local authority (social care). Many changes have been made to the statutory services in the recent past. Successive governments across the political spectrum have required these services to modernise, streamline and increase the level of quality. It has been a long process, with many staff feeling the constant pressure of change. Despite the changes, occupational therapists continue to lead innovative practice in these sectors and it is unlikely that occupational therapists would not have a role in these areas in the future.

The National Health Service (NHS)

The NHS has many different services where occupational therapists can be found. Acute and foundation hospitals provide essential care for people who need emergency care or who have planned medical interventions. Occupational therapists can be found right at the heart of emergency care, working in the Accident and Emergency (A&E) department assessing individuals to see if it is possible to avoid a hospital admission through the provision of rehabilitation equipment and safety advice. Occupational therapists work on the medical, surgical, orthopaedic and mental health wards, in paediatrics, hand clinics, wheelchair services, stroke teams, burns and plastic surgery and long-term conditions. They are also heavily involved in intermediate care and other community-based teams. Intermediate care is a service where, as well as trying to prevent unnecessary admissions, the occupational therapists also work to speed up the discharges through the provision of alternative support mechanisms. Occupational therapists are also involved in end of life care, working in palliative care and on regional teams for illnesses such as HIV and AIDS.

There are so many different areas where occupational therapists are employed within the NHS. Sometimes there is an occupational therapy department, with assessment and treatment facilities and office space. This is used as a base and the occupational therapists see their service users on the wards, only bringing them to the department for specific interventions. In other areas occupational therapists work within inter-professional teams. This is when a group of different professionals work in a team, generally with a specific service user group – for example an intermediate care team – working from a shared base. Some teams are a mixture of NHS staff and social services staff, who work together to ensure the best service for their service users. An example of joint working in this way is a learning disability team.

The NHS provides free care at the point of need. Occupational therapists will nevertheless, become involved in assessing needs and making recommendations with regard to equipment provision. As well as assessing and treating the service users, reports need to be written, records kept and liaison with other members of the inter-professional team maintained. These other activities can take up considerable time and are an essential part of the role. Occupational therapists are sometimes assisted by occupational therapy assistants, technical instructors or generic assistants. The occupational therapist must learn how to prioritise their work and delegate specific tasks to other members of the team. In addition to the assessments and treatment interventions that are undertaken within the hospital, occupational therapists are often required to undertake home assessments. The occupational therapist carries out a series of assessments in the service user's home, sometimes environmental assessments and other times with the service user, checking their safety and independence. This is when the occupational therapist's ability to problem-solve is especially valuable.

The following case studies aim to give some insight into a selection of occupational therapy roles in the NHS. Unfortunately there is not enough space in an introductory book like this to include every kind of team or service in detail – hopefully those that have been chosen will help you to put occupational therapy into perspective. In addition, we have included some longer examples of a day in the life of some occupational therapists in a new chapter at the end of this book. As an occupational therapist you will have a variety of different roles to fulfil regardless of the setting in which you work. These examples will give a flavour of that variety and the tasks to be completed.

Case study: Working in mental health services for older people – John Payne

'As a band 5 Occupational Therapist working in Mental Health Older Persons services my days are busy and fulfilling. I am influenced by the work of Tom Kitwood. He developed the theory of personhood; his approaches, ideas and concepts dictate how I interact with clients and understand their needs.

The main role of the occupational therapist is to conduct functional performance assessments with clients who are diagnosed with a mental health problem or an organic illness. I complete a minimum of two home assessments per week. I arrange a home visit and follow a person, environment, occupation model. My assessments are thorough, looking at such areas as: the routines of the individual, mobility, and perhaps the most important factor: how their illness has impacted on their life. I also complete the Large Allan Cognitive Screening Tool. This standardised evidence-based assessment allows me to understand how dementia can impact upon a person's occupational performance.

Once the assessment is written I implement my recommendations and intervention plan. These are often diverse reflecting my holistic approach. I deliver interventions around psycho-social needs including: community access and kitchen assessments. I may prescribe appropriate adaptive equipment to address physical needs or I may refer the client to a relevant service. I promote personhood and participation in life story work, which can help the family to better understand their relative.

I deliver cognitive stimulation therapy, a 14 session programme for people diagnosed with early to middle stage dementia. I facilitate the group in collaboration with support workers. This includes planning sessions, inviting clients, steering the group and keeping appropriate records. We ensure the therapy is informal and stimulating.

Being a positive member of the multidisciplinary team is crucial in the role. It helps to build professional working relationships and, crucially, advocates the varied services occupational therapists can provide.'

Case study: Working in a surgical ward – Katy Langford

'I work on an acute hospital ward covering patients admitted for surgical procedures. Some surgeries can be relatively routine, meaning that there is no need for occupational therapy input, whilst others result in considerable changes for patients to cope with – and our role becomes complex. This can be challenging; you need to be able to prioritise patients with very different needs and circumstances.

There may be a psychological impact for patients undergoing surgery. For example, patients who have had a limb amputated, a stoma bag fitted, or a mastectomy, may have a change in body image, and grieve the loss of these body parts in conjunction with limitations on physical mobility and general functioning. As occupational therapists, we are holistic, and need to consider these effects when working with patients to devise a treatment plan. Aspects of this may include referring patients into mental health services or other agencies for more specialised support.

The treatment plan may be very functional, such as assessing how a patient manages transfers and day to day tasks such as washing, dressing and meal preparation or providing basic rehabilitation equipment to aid them once they return home. I am also responsible for assessing the suitability of a patient's current property for them to return back to, working with social services to find them more suitable accommodation and considering essential adaptations.

Working on a surgical ward is extremely varied and fast paced – patients may only be referred into the service a day or two before they are expected to return home. There are challenges in terms of time management, understanding the complex relationship between several medical conditions and the psychosocial impact. All of these factors make it an interesting and rewarding area to work in.'

Every area of practice is different – the following is an example of what the therapist does when working with an individual client.

Case study: Working in mental health – Wendy Ferguson

'As an occupational therapist working in an NHS foundation trust, I have worked with people of all ages with a wide range of mental health needs, people who sometimes have physical health needs too.

In the course of my career this has included working with older people and working-aged people with dementia as well as people of all ages experiencing difficulty getting on with their daily lives due to anxiety, depression and psychosis.

Helping people to manage their symptoms and to live their lives at home, work and out and about within their communities involves working closely with the person themselves and their carers to identify the steps they need to take to achieve their personal aspirations.

To ensure that people get the right specialist help to meet their complex needs, mental health occupational therapists work closely with other professionals in inpatient and community teams including nurses, social workers, psychologists, psychiatrists and a range of allied health professionals including physiotherapists and art therapists.

Susan had been referred to the mental health team having become very socially isolated due to longstanding anxiety and depression. She rarely left her house and relied on relatives to do her weekly shopping. Susan also had osteoarthritis which made it difficult for her to manage daily activities in her home.

Through discussion with Susan she identified that she had always enjoyed reading and painting but had lost motivation to continue to do these activities in recent times.

We devised a plan together to enable her to be able to manage her daily activities at home more easily and the small pieces of equipment she tried helped her to manage bathing, dressing and kitchen tasks with less pain and fatigue.

Following this Susan felt more motivated to take part in an art group at a local community arts centre and, with graded support, gradually got back to using local buses to get there.

Before being discharged from the team, Susan devised her personal recovery action plan to help her stay well and identified strategies and coping skills she could use on a daily basis to maintain good mental and physical health and cope with any future downturns in her mental health. She eventually also joined a local book club too.'

In this example, it is clear how the occupational therapist's intervention has led to a resolution of the difficulties experienced by the client. This appears to be quite straightforward. There are some problems identified by the client and the therapist and so they work together to resolve them. Occupational therapists will also work in more complex situations where this will involve colleagues from the multidisciplinary team. The team will need to communicate effectively to maintain continuity of care and resolution of a range of problems.

Case study: Working in medicine – Gemma Pratt

'As an occupational therapist working in medicine the main aim of my role is to facilitate a safe and timely discharge home from hospital.

Many of the patients on the ward present with diverse and often complex physical and psychological conditions, therefore when I receive a referral I begin by gathering information on that person's presenting medical condition(s) and their past medical history by accessing medical records and attending multidisciplinary ward handovers. I then complete an initial assessment with the patient to establish their previous/current functional abilities as well as gathering information on their home circumstances, and work with them to form a goal orientated treatment plan. The main assessments completed in this area are washing and dressing/kitchen/cognition/mobility and transfer assessments and home visits. The outcomes of these assessments are used to determine if the patient is able to return home independently, or if they require a further rehabilitation/care package or 24 hour care placement.

Working in this environment requires you to be flexible and adaptable as things can evolve and change as the day goes on, for example changes in patients' medical status following a consultant ward round, or a change in discharge destination, so it's imperative that you have good time management skills and are able to prioritise your caseload effectively, which includes being able to delegate work to assistants as appropriate.

Listening to the patients' wishes and seeking to understand their priorities helps to demonstrate dignified and person centred care. Developing skills in advocacy and negotiation are essential for occupational therapists in this role.'

The following example from Wheelchair Services further demonstrates the importance of the intervention being based around the specific needs of the client.

Case study: Working in Wheelchair Services – Judith Hallett

'Working in Wheelchair Services offers me the opportunity to work with individuals to ensure they have the right sort of wheelchair and all of the correct adaptations and accessories. Some of my service users come for a short-term loan while others have a lifelong connection with the service, as I continue to assess and advise them as their condition alters over time. The following short case study is one aspect of my work.

John aged 55 years has multiple sclerosis, he cannot walk and his sitting balance is poor. His arms are weak and sometimes he has involuntary movements of them. John lives in a small bungalow with his wife. She helps him with most activities of daily living and pushes him around the bungalow in a wheelchair. They live in a remote village and his wife does not drive. John was referred by his doctor for assessment for a powered indoor wheelchair.

I carried out a home visit and assessed John for an indoor powered wheelchair. He could drive this chair around his bungalow and transfer from it independently onto his bed and toilet. Space in the home was quite limited but he and his wife were prepared to change the furniture to make manoeuvring the chair easier. John's sitting balance was poor and he had to hold on to the arms of the chair constantly to maintain his posture – this led to him struggling to feed himself and move his arms to carry out any activity. I assessed him for a postural cushion which had wedges down the side and a pommel. This supportive cushion fixed his pelvis and enabled him to move his arms more freely. The access to his bungalow was poor and his wife struggled to get his manual wheelchair down the two steps at the front door – the back door had four steps. I made a referral to social services for a ramp at the front door. Once this has been completed I will assess John for an indoor/outdoor powered chair. This will give him access to the local community and he will be able to use wheelchair accessible taxis and buses to travel further if he wants.'

Occupational therapists sometimes work in secure settings, which adds a different dimension to the working environment and will involve complex risk assessments.

Case study: Working in forensic mental health – Kelly Peare

'Working as an occupational therapist within a forensic setting is unique; in addition to having a diagnosis of a mental health condition, the people I work with have also been in contact, in some way, with the criminal justice system. This can bring additional challenges, in terms of greater stigmatisation, often poorer family support, and a lengthier stay in hospital. The latter can become a positive for both the individual and the therapist; I believe this longer timescale allows for building strong therapeutic alliances, motivating individuals to achieve their personal life goals.

The chance to bring your own personal interests to the role is a huge positive. Forensic services can be seen as a restrictive environment; environmental considerations are massive, hence the value of therapeutic use of self can never be underestimated. As an occupational therapist you soon become accustomed to using plastic cutlery, and inventing innovative approaches to cooking assessments. Assessment is the primary focus of occupational therapy, to gain an insight into the strengths and needs of each individual, alongside the influences of a restrictive environment and the consequent impact upon quality of life.

The secondary focus is on early engagement; each of the forensic wards has a clear and distinct specialism, and as a result the occupational therapy approach used in each reflects the specific requirements of the individuals and therefore guides the interventions offered.

My work requires a highly dynamic approach; balancing therapy and risk can be very rewarding especially when you dynamically risk assess in collaboration with individuals meaning you are truly person-centred. Assessment through activity feels like you are always engaging your patients in something meaningful to them; whilst I facilitate a range of interventions to enable structure and constructive use of time, there is opportunity to explore new interests, which is enlightening to see.'

Occupational therapists also work in end of life care, with service users and carers, at a very emotional time.

Case study: Working in palliative care – Nicola Simpson

'Working as a Macmillan Occupational Therapist allows me the opportunity to work with patients and their carers in their own home, at a very difficult time. I work with patients at a time when their life is often being taken over by their disease and all too often, they are losing their life roles. I believe that by helping people to engage in activities which are meaningful and pleasurable to them, I have the opportunity to assist them in achieving their goals, improving their quality of life and giving them back a sense of control and achievement.

One of the patients I worked with had bowel cancer with lung and liver metastases and was struggling with cancer related fatigue. This was limiting his ability to engage in his usual leisure and social activities and his motivation was reduced. By working in partnership with him and his wife, focusing on prioritising, planning, pacing and goal setting, he was able to start going out of the house again. He achieved his goal of going to his local golf club with his wife, to use the driving range and eat lunch. This gave him a sense of achievement and increased his motivation and confidence.'

Local authority

Working within local authority social services is a fast-paced community environment, which involves working with service users in their own homes. Occupational therapists are employed within teams to provide assessments aimed at reducing risk and maintaining independence for service users. This may involve the assessment for and provision of equipment to help maintain independence and safety as well as undertaking assessments and advising on major adaptations to properties, to allow them to be accessible for a service user with a disability. As with NHS work, occupational therapists will find themselves working with service users who have long-term conditions as well as urgent needs. Although working in a team, there is a great amount of lone working too.

The complexities of practice are found in all areas. The following case study demonstrates something of these complexities which are exacerbated by the cultural, political and legal implications of this area of practice.

Case study: Working in primary care – Claire Smith

'People seeking asylum were a totally new group for me to work with when I applied for a post in a GP surgery specialising in meeting the needs of refugees. I had worked in mental health day services, and later in education, since I qualified, and had lived and worked in areas of very limited diversity. The post was for a "psychological therapist" rather than specifically an occupational therapist -- but it occurred to me as an opportunity to work with a very marginalised group of people, work in a primary care setting, and meet a very broad range of needs across a variety of cultural groups. It has proved to be all that, and more.

The first thing that struck me was how familiar people's needs are, wherever they are from – their hopes, wishes and fears were just the same as anyone else's, in spite of being faced with often extreme circumstances. The diversity of life experience was staggering, but people were invariably struggling with issues of loss, adjustment to their new environment, and fear of the future.

For some people, they were looking for the chance to meet someone with a listening ear, who would hear their story, take them seriously and allow them the chance to share their feelings. For others they were looking for the opportunity to develop strategies for managing day to day life while awaiting a decision about their future.

While judgements are made by the UK Border Agency about whether someone who claims asylum has the right to stay here in the UK, the person has very limited rights and opportunities. They are not allowed to work, have very limited access to education (including English courses) and have no choice about where they can live. Finances are tight as they receive 70% of income support, so many aspects of everyday living can be very restricted. As well as these practical challenges, they may feel very isolated – away from family, networks and community and surrounded by the unfamiliar. They have skills and resources that are rarely tapped into, and find themselves progressively de-skilled by their prolonged wait.

Occupational therapy can provide a bridge between the old life and the new, helping people to manage the transition and find a meaningful way of living in the here and now while a decision is pending. Understanding what is important to the individual, how they expressed themselves before they came to the UK can give you clues as to how they might best adapt to life here – trying to recreate roles, relationships and activities that previously had meaning for them.

It can involve signposting people towards opportunities in their local community – perhaps a singing class, or an informal English lesson – or perhaps finding things which help with daily tasks, like a food shop that stocks traditional produce. It can also be about helping the person see their own capabilities and resources – the asylum process tends to make people feel very passive and disconnected, so helping them to acknowledge their own resourcefulness and capability can empower them to help themselves and those around them.

If someone is lucky enough to be granted asylum status, they have a massive change ahead – they have the opportunity to begin a new life, which is exciting and daunting, and is coupled with the loss of home and family. They suddenly need to find a new home, find work and establish themselves as a UK citizen. So much of this process is occupational, so help in negotiating this change and managing the process is tremendously helpful. Where people have developed meaningful networks and relationships during the wait for a decision these often stand the person in good stead, maintaining their well-being and their sense of self ready for the new start.

If they are not granted asylum they live in fear of deportation, with the removal of financial support. This can be a tremendously challenging time, where we can only hope that meaningful networks they established before can help to support them, and a positive relationship with their therapist might make them feel they are not alone.

So, for me it has been a tough area of practice, working against a complex and challenging legal background and facing real and significant need; but it has also been fantastically varied and brought me into contact with people I might never have had the pleasure to meet otherwise. Helping people to connect here in the UK either to their "old selves" or new ones, finding a meaningful way to spend their time, and supporting people who otherwise get very little, felt like a valuable occupational therapy contribution to a growing potential practice area.'

Inter-professional working

All professionals working with service users are encouraged to work inter-professionally. This means that they come together sharing their skills and expertise to ensure that the best possible plan of interventions are made for each individual service user. Throughout your training to become an occupational therapist you will be encouraged to find out about the other professions that occupational therapists work alongside. Both in training and once you are in practice you will get the opportunity to work with such professionals and develop your skills together. It is important to understand the different roles and value each other's contribution to good service delivery.

Case study: Working in intermediate care – Kim Cale

'While being an occupational therapist on a physical rotation an unexpected opportunity came up for me to step across into community working – which was where I had always hoped to develop my career further.

Working in intermediate care has provided me with an endless supply of learning opportunities and life experiences that have enabled me to consolidate existing skills, and incorporate new ones gained through work based training and self-directed learning.

Intermediate care provides rehabilitation activities within a time specific, goal orientated approach. My clients are of adult age, with a range of rehabilitation needs including long-term conditions, trauma, stroke, falls, and delirium, to name a few. One day I could be teaching a client with multiple sclerosis coping strategies – while preparing a meal for their family, and the next be providing equipment for a client with an amputation – enabling them to shower independently.

Assessments and treatment are delivered on a one to one basis or within groups, and delivered in settings such as a person's own home, supported living complexes and nursing homes where they can be temporarily placed – if temporarily placed, my role expands to facilitating a safe discharge home, providing reablement activities to promote independence.

Being an occupational therapist in intermediate care allows me to be a creative, holistic practitioner and has given me the chance to be involved in ongoing service development activities.

From being a lone occupational therapist within the service – I am proud to say we are now a visionary team of six occupational therapists and for me, this feels very exciting – as our occupational therapy role continues to evolve and grow to become an integral part of community life for all who work and use the service.'

Chapter summary

There are so many different opportunities in the statutory sector, which is traditionally where occupational therapists have been employed. Although there have been major changes to the contemporary landscape of the National Health Service and social care, there is still a requirement for occupational therapy. You may find yourself involved with service improvement initiatives or setting up new services, which is very exciting. The occupational therapists who have shared their experiences in this book have had careers of varying lengths, however their energy and enthusiasm for the work they do is still as high as it was when they first qualified. They continue to be inspirational.

Key points

- Statutory services provide a wide variety of opportunities for occupational therapists.
- Often there will be a significant number of occupational therapists working in larger organisations so there is a professional community for support.

Useful resources

The College of Occupational Therapists: www.cot.co.uk

Chapter 12

Occupational therapy in the non-statutory sector

BPP UNIVERSITY SCHOOL OF HEALTH

The opportunities for occupational therapists to work outside the statutory sector have increased dramatically over recent years. While working practices may be very similar to those experienced within health and social services the context of practice may be focused on different perspectives.

When you have gained a degree of experience and feel that you would like to work for yourself there is the possibility of functioning as an independent practitioner. This will make a whole new set of demands of you which may not have been included in your initial training as an occupational therapist and the decision should not be taken lightly. You will have to maintain records of not only your client contacts but also the records of your business. This will require you to develop a new set of information technology skills. This may involve the use of databases and spreadsheets as you will be required to set up your own accounts and manage your own caseload and business contacts. You may need to develop your business planning. It will be necessary to seek funding for your work, seek out suppliers and develop less expensive strategies for interventions which will be more efficient. This role will allow you to see the strengths and limitations of working in the statutory sector. You can determine which clients you want to work with and how you want to develop your professional skills. Whilst there are many advantages to this role you will also need to recognise the changes required. There will be no sick pay. If you are not well you will not get paid. There are no pension rights and you may have to consider this separately. There are no guarantees in private practice but there are a great many opportunities that many find particularly rewarding.

This chapter will briefly consider some of these areas and offer insight and experience to help you consider future career opportunities.

Case study: Independent practitioner – Helen McCloughry

'When I trained as an occupational therapist I had no idea or plan that I would end up running my own management consultancy. It was when I completed my Master's degree that my tutor advised me to look for management roles. At the time I was working as a community occupational therapist.

An opportunity arose to conduct a small project looking at placing occupational therapy skills within the social work teams. The project was quickly able to demonstrate the impact of "reablement", as it is now called. I found that my training in skills analysis was easily transferable to project management. This led straight away to being invited to manage another project that later became known as intermediate care. At the heart of these projects was the hypothesis that occupational therapy's approach to independence was more effective and better value for money than traditional service models.

An opportunity then arose for me to further develop and manage this service but, this time from the NHS, so I moved across as Head of Service. Being in a leadership and management position enabled me to influence commissioning decisions and build an integrated community service for adults where therapists were able to play a central role. Throughout my career I have also found that occupational therapy is uniquely placed as a bridge between both social and medical worldviews. This perspective has enabled me to combine strategic planning with my core skills of problem-solving. Having an "enabling" approach to management also empowers staff to deliver their best.

Finally, as Assistant Director, and building on lessons learnt from developing intermediate care services, I was able to continue to join up services across health and social care.

All of this experience enabled me to develop my business management skills. When I linked this to my occupational therapy knowledge I was able to spot a gap in the market and develop my own consultancy business, MS Squared Consulting. Through this business I offer independent advice and guidance to organisations wishing to integrate their services, especially when resources are scarce.'

Working independently will have its challenges but this will appeal to many therapists who wish to be able to manage their own time and also reap the rewards of working for themselves. There are other opportunities for working in other ways. The following case shows the benefits of working within the charitable sector.

Case study: Charitable sector – Linsey Smith

'I work part time for a local authority. I also work part time in independent practice. Currently, I am working on an exciting business project with Heel and Toe Children's Charity which is based in Framwellgate Moor, Durham City.

I met with the trustees, the Charity Manager and the Service Development Manager following a visit to the charity to learn more about their service. We all discovered that we share the same vision, which is to develop a children's and adults' therapy service. This would include occupational therapy, conductive education, physiotherapy, counselling, psychotherapy, speech and language therapy as well as other disciplines. We set up regular meetings to discuss and develop working terms as well as create a business plan.

I am working as a self-employed consultant for the service and charity at present with the aim to create full-time salaried positions not only for me, but for other professionals. At present our professional associates are not "employed" but are "self-employed", as this is how we have chosen to reduce overheads to support start up. What makes this project really exciting is our business model. Yes, it is a business; yes, we want to make a profit but a large percentage of our profits will be donated to the charity to fund service developments and create salaried positions for allied health professionals. We really want a service that is free at the point of delivery for all who access it.

We hear the term "think outside of the box" in the profession of occupational therapy. This project has certainly and continues to challenge my thinking. How did this all start? The answer is social media. I use social media to network, to talk and engage with other professionals who have similar interests for professional networking.'

While this is run as a business there are other opportunities to give back to the charity itself. Other businesses will use a traditional model and there are many opportunities for therapists to work in this way. In the next case John demonstrates how being an occupational therapist in private practice is very similar to functioning in the traditional areas of practice.

Case study: Private practice – John Pope

'The private unit I work for provides specialist care for adults between 18 and 65 years of age with needs such as learning disabilities, challenging behaviour, autistic spectrum disorder, a diagnosed mental illness and also dual diagnosis of any of these conditions. The focus of Huntercombe House is towards rehabilitation that will provide individuals with the encouragement they need to ultimately return to a less supported environment and, where possible, their own tenancy.

As part of the multidisciplinary team (which consists of nursing, psychology and psychiatry), the occupational therapy service ensures the rehabilitation plans remain meaningful and client-centred.

The main roles of the occupational therapist include:

- Occupational therapy assessments – including an activities of daily living assessment on admission to the home.
- Intervention sessions based on the need, these can be one to one or group sessions. Common areas include cooking skills, sensory sessions, laundry skills and shopping skills.
- Assisting in the writing of care plans, risk assessments and behaviour plans to ensure the individual clients have the opportunities they need for rehabilitation. Occupational therapy leads care planning for all activities of daily living.
- Working with the Personal Activities Leader to ensure activity timetables reflect the intervention needs.
- Ensuring individual clients have access to wider community facilities for example, leisure interests, education courses, voluntary opportunities.

Following assessment, the intervention plans are developed to enable the individual clients to develop their skills ready for a move back into a less-supported environment. While at our unit, individual clients receive one to one support from members of the staff. I work closely with the staff to ensure they understand the needs of the individual clients and to ensure that the work they do is focused on independence. I attend meetings with the keyworker teams which allow me to work with the staff on goal setting to ensure the individual clients progress to achieve their aims.

The unique role of occupational therapy within a residential setting enables individual clients to develop their skills and ensure the meaning of "independence" remains. I have found my skills as an occupational therapist are being utilised in many different ways. There is definite scope for occupational therapists working in this environment and this should be celebrated.'

New areas of independent practice

One increasingly popular area for independent practice has come in response to the Government's welfare reform agenda and attitudes to Personal Independence Payments. This has resulted in a great number of individuals being assessed to determine the amount of funding they might receive in order to help with the extra costs caused by a disability or long-term ill-health. As this payment is determined by the way a condition affects the individual engaging in activities of daily living rather than the condition itself this means that everyone must be considered independently. This will require you, as a therapist, to assess the individual and complete a legal report which will support the claimant through their benefit journey. This may require you to work evenings and weekends as this meets the circumstances of the client group. You would usually work with clients in their own home.

Another more established area for practice is that of vocational rehabilitation. This has been defined as 'whatever helps someone with a health problem to stay at, return to and remain in work' (Waddell, Burton, Kendall, 2008). This has become increasingly important within the profession and has led to the College of Occupational Therapists producing a brief guide in conjunction with its specialist section. This work responds to the government drivers to reduce the benefits bill and increase the number of people available to work. One of the core elements of our profession has always been about workplace skills and whilst this is only part of our practice it remains a key aspect of what occupational therapists are trained to do.

The College of Occupational Therapists has produced two key documents to help clarify the role of the occupational therapist – *Work Matters: Vocational Navigation for Occupational Therapy Staff* (2007) helps staff to develop effective partnerships, the second document is The College of Occupational Therapists' *Vocational Rehabilitation Strategy* (2008) which sets out its belief that 'everyone in the UK has the right to information, help and support to be able to work, whether this is paid employment, voluntary work or work to care for family or home.' (COT, 2008, p.1)

This role will consist of a holistic approach to working with the client. It will consider physical, social and psychological needs. As this work is normally referred through insurance companies or employers there can be a wide range of intervention opportunities. Your involvement will normally encompass a series of assessments of the individual, the workplace and the demands of the work role. This will result in the development of a work plan which will include the strategies for the individual's rehabilitation and incorporate the timescales progress points and expectations in the return to work strategy. As with other areas of independent or non-statutory work there will be a demand for autonomous and highly motivated individuals who have lots of experience, have developed specialist skills and have a desire for self-development.

Chapter summary

While this area of practice offers a range of differences to the statutory sector the role of the occupational therapist remains very similar. The intervention process remains the same and the therapist will draw upon the same skills as well as developing a new set of skills around managing or adapting to a different model of relating to the client group. While the case studies in this chapter have offered some examples of occupational therapy practice they barely scratch the surface of what therapists might achieve. The following chapter will consider the international perspective of occupational therapy.

Key points

- The possibilities are endless in this sector.
- Advice about business and financial issues will be essential.

Useful resources

College of Occupational Therapists Specialist Section – Independent Practice: www.cotss-ip.org.uk/

College of Occupational Therapists (2008) *The College of Occupational Therapists' Vocational Rehabilitation Strategy*. London: COT.

Waddell, G, Burton, AK, Kendall, NAS (2008) *Vocational rehabilitation: what works, for whom, and when?* London: Stationery Office.

Chapter 13

International perspectives

BPP
UNIVERSITY
SCHOOL OF HEALTH

In its first 100 years occupational therapy has grown and developed, impacting on countries across the world. During this period it has been supported by a network of national professional bodies and organisations. In 1952 ten national organisations agreed to a constitution of the World Federation of Occupational Therapists (WFOT). Its original objectives included:

- To act as the official international organisation for the promotion of occupational therapy
- To promote international co-operation among occupational therapy associations, therapists and other allied professional groups
- To advance the practice and standards of occupational therapy
- To help maintain the ethics and to advance the interests of the profession
- To facilitate the international exchange and placements of therapists and students
- To facilitate the exchange of information
- To promote the education and training of therapists
- To hold international congresses

By 1963 WFOT was recognised as a Non-Governmental Organisation (NGO) by the United Nations (UN). Affiliation with this organisation is important for all occupational therapists. Its member organisations now represent over 350,000 occupational therapists around the world. Participating fully in WFOT activity opens great opportunities for therapists. With a focus on the development and training for emerging areas of occupational therapy practice and support for disaster relief across the world, there is always much to do.

When considering your training in the United Kingdom make sure that you enrol on a programme which is accredited by the College of Occupational Therapists as this ensures that your qualification is accepted by the WFOT. With this international recognition it is much easier to practise occupational therapy around the world, although as mentioned in Chapter 10 there will still be some local requirements which must be met.

In addition to the worldwide perspectives, occupational therapists have the support of the Council of Occupational Therapists for the European Countries (COTEC). COTEC was established with the purpose of co-ordinating the views of national associations of occupational therapy to enable them to work together to develop and improve standards of professional practice and education, to harmonise the work of member associations and to advance the theory of the profession across Europe. In addition, COTEC aims to enable and promote the movement of individual occupational therapists within Europe and increase the profile of the profession. COTEC represents 27 European occupational therapy associations and more than 120,000 occupational therapists.

The strong international links help the profession to better support the changing demands of a worldwide population. It is not uncommon for international students to come to the United Kingdom to study. This might be enrolling on one of the courses already mentioned in Chapter 3 or it might be about updating or enhancing previous studies. For some this is completing additional work to top up a Diploma in Occupational Therapy or completing studies at Master's level in order to seek opportunities more easily in the international job market. Some countries require different registration requirements which new graduates need to be made aware of.

Case study: Working abroad – Tina Gericke

'Few professions enable you to work abroad so easily. To date, I have worked as an occupational therapist in South Africa, Canada, Australia, America, Italy and Macedonia, as well as in the UK.

Increasingly occupational therapy is becoming a profession that crosses international borders. It is fast developing a common professional culture with a common language and common tools. One such tool is the International Classification of Functioning, Disability and Health (ICF) produced by the World Health Organisation. The ICF provides a framework to view and intervene to minimise the effects of disability. It recognises that activity and participation are key outcomes of any intervention. It also acknowledges that personal factors particularly personal motivation, and the environment, physical and people environment, impacts hugely on the outcome of any intervention – all core elements of occupational therapy.

The area of disability is not the only one in which occupational therapists work. At a recent European conference, there were presentations from around the world about emerging areas of practice, for example working with asylum seekers and with homeless war veterans. At that same conference there were occupational therapists not just from Western Europe, America, Canada and Australia but also from some of the ex-Soviet Union countries, Iran, Iraq, Taiwan, and Japan.

> We are so lucky that the common language between all these countries is English. So while there will be challenges to working internationally, the communication bridges are there.
>
> At what point in your career might it be good to work abroad? You might be interested to go as a student and do a clinical practice placement overseas as part of an exchange programme. You might decide to work abroad when you first qualify, as I did, joining a rotation scheme for new graduates at a Cape Town hospital. After two or three years as a qualified occupational therapist, once you've developed your professional identity and feel secure of your skills, you would be eligible to work with some of the charities, such as Voluntary Service Overseas (VSO), who recruit occupational therapists to work in the less well-resourced parts of the world. You might one day, like me, choose to work overseas towards the end of your professional career, to exchange and share some of the knowledge accumulated over the years, and mentor therapists from the newly emerging occupational therapy schools around the world. The NHS now recognise that there are mutual benefits to supporting staff who wish to work in less well-resourced countries for a period. As a qualified occupational therapist, the world can be your oyster.'

As a student, there are often opportunities to engage with students from other countries. The Erasmus+ programme supports education and training with organisations that seek to enhance the learning experience of their students.

Erasmus+ can provide funding to allow participants to pursue stimulating learning opportunities across Europe. This may mean that there are opportunities to study elsewhere in Europe and learn on the programmes of partner universities. This will help you to develop your transferable skills. There will be increased opportunities to develop your international view of occupational therapy but also appreciate the cultural differences which might exist across Europe.

This might be something you can discuss at interview or once you have commenced your programme of studies.

For many, there is an interest in working overseas. The countries which are most often considered are the USA, Canada, Australia and New Zealand. Having your degree in occupational therapy will not always be enough for this transition. This section will indicate the type of expectations which must be met to work in some of these countries.

The American Occupational Therapy Association requires a post professional Master's degree in occupational therapy or a pre-registration Master's degree to be considered to take the certification exam. Those who have qualified with a Bachelor's degree would have some additional work to do prior to applying. They would then also need to successfully complete the certification exam. The applicant would also need appropriate visa clearance and ensure they meet the state regulatory requirements of the state in which they wish to practise.

The application process for working is Canada is similar. Those who gained their qualification outside of Canada must contact the Association of Canadian Occupational Therapy Regulatory Organizations and complete an assessment process which ensures equivalency in your qualification. When you have successfully demonstrated this you will then be given access to additional assessments to ensure that you have the basic practice competencies and the legal understanding to practise in Canada.

Other countries will have similar expectations to ensure that any international therapists have been fully prepared to work in their adopted country. With this wealth of opportunities available it may give you something to consider as you complete your training as an occupational therapist and inspire you to take advantage of any additional learning opportunities to enhance your personal portfolio.

Case study: Perspectives of an international occupational therapist – Verena Langlotz Kondzic

'One of the reasons I chose to become an occupational therapist was the chance to easily work in another country. Being part of a smaller profession worldwide has the advantage that there is a special kinship between occupational therapists from different countries, often referred to as the occupational therapy family.

Some universities provide possibilities for students to go on placements abroad during your undergraduate studies. Staying overseas can foster intercultural competencies by learning about values, health understandings and cultural beliefs of other fellow human beings. To acquire these competencies becomes more and more crucial for occupational therapists as personal beliefs and individual values stand at the core of our work and it is a reality that many of our patients have a migrant background. Research has shown that the immersion into another culture is not enough to expand our cultural learnings but additionally it is important to have a cultural mentor who helps us to understand the other culture and reframe the experience and beliefs in order to expand our understanding. This is an exciting undertaking and in return will need a curious mind and a flexible approach.

As I didn't have the opportunity to go on a placement abroad during my undergraduate studies I secured a postgraduate placement in Australia through my own initiative to learn how occupational therapy is practised there and to gain a better understanding of the English occupational therapy terminology, as this is not my native language. Two years later, while working in a spinal cord rehabilitation centre, I took the chance to join an international Non-Governmental Organisation to deliver and adapt 170 wheelchairs to persons with disabilities in Mongolia for two weeks. I had read about the opportunity on the Website of the World Federation of Occupational Therapists (WFOT). This gave me a small glimpse into another culture and its people and marked the beginning of a long-term involvement which led to a WFOT supported project to establish Occupational Therapy in Mongolia. Years later, continuing the collaboration between the Mongolian and my Swiss university has become part of my job as an international co-ordinator and lecturer.

My experience is just one of many. I have met colleagues who have worked abroad on short projects or for longer periods of time or choose to stay in a new country permanently. The profession in many countries is on the list of desirable visa applicants, and occupational therapists are actively encouraged to seek job opportunities. There is also a high need for occupational therapists in the many countries where the profession is still developing and in exchange the application process is often easier. Occupational therapy social media platforms offer quick and informal approaches to seek international work next to the official contacts of the countries' national associations. It is recommended and in some cases mandatory to gain two years of experience prior to working abroad. There are many opportunities for future occupational therapists to join international projects and services be they government run or privately initiated. Becoming an occupational therapist is a first step to combine exploring the world and empowering people in need.'

Chapter summary

The international focus within occupational therapy programmes may vary; however, you can be assured that the College of Occupational Therapists is committed to working with its European and worldwide colleagues to ensure that occupational therapy is used to its potential to help individuals. The world feels a smaller place with the increase in technology and improvement in available low cost transport. You can play an active part in providing occupational therapy in both developed and developing countries, share good practice and bring home new ideas.

Key points

- There are many organisations who offer long- and short-term placements in a wide variety of countries.
- Positions are available for paid employment and voluntary work.
- Some countries will require you to take further examinations or to have a Master's degree.

Useful resources

Department of Health (2010) *The Framework for NHS Involvement in International Development.* London: Crown.

International Classification of Functioning, Disability and Health: www.who.int/classifications/icf/en/

Voluntary Services Overseas: www.vso.org.uk/volunteer

Outreach International: www.outreachinternational.co.uk/

Chapter 14

A day in the life – occupational therapy in action

BPP UNIVERSITY SCHOOL OF HEALTH

In this chapter we have provided eight examples provided by highly skilled occupational therapists working in different areas of practice. Nothing can replace spending time shadowing an occupational therapist, which would allow you the opportunity to ask questions – but hopefully these case studies will provide you with an insight, enabling you to finalise your career choice. There is also a snapshot into a typical Monday at university, so that you can see what might be expected of you there.

Case study: Working in older age medicine – Katy Williams

'This case is typical of those seen by an occupational therapist working on Medical Elderly wards where patients often have a combination of long standing ailments and newly diagnosed ones, or an increase in severity of an existing problem. Illness can affect the individual's physical ability, level of function and mental health.

Mrs Hall is 87 years old. Police are called to her house and find her on the floor; an ambulance takes her to Accident and Emergency (A&E). She is extremely dehydrated, there is evidence of a urine infection, her blood sugar is low and her heartbeat and breathing are slightly irregular. She is admitted to an acute medical ward. A course of antibiotics clears her urine infection; diet and medication bring her blood sugar and heart rate under control. She is still short of breath upon exertion. Cardiac failure and diabetes are diagnosed. Medical staff declared her medically fit for discharge.

On the ward Mrs Hall is settled at night, getting out of bed to use the commode once or twice in the early hours. She manages this by herself. In the morning, some prompting is needed to get her out of bed. Supervision and prompting is also required for her to wash and dress herself. Given a bowl of water or left in the bathroom Mrs Hall begins to wash herself but tends to lose concentration. Mrs Hall's appetite is poor and her weight is low. She needs to eat and drink adequately, but prompting by staff is required at mealtimes. Some reddened areas are apparent on her heels and shoulders. She sleeps on a low level pressure mattress on the ward and has a pressure cushion on her chair. Mrs Hall requires a walking frame and can only manage short distances before tiring. She struggles to get to the toilet at the end of the ward and incontinence becomes a problem. "Accidents" distress her so nurses tend to take the commode to her and provide pads which seems to reduce her anxiety. Mrs Hall tells staff if the pads need changing but requires help to put a dry pad on. Despite the infection being cleared Mrs Hall is still mildly confused; she appears to be more muddled when tired, but she hasn't wandered off the ward.

Mrs Hall wants to go back to her home. It is the occupational therapist's job to ensure that she will be safe if she does. A thorough assessment of her physical ability, cognition and her ability to perform day to day tasks is undertaken to identify the potential consequences of a change to her functional level and solutions need to be found. The occupational therapist liaises with other members of the multidisciplinary hospital team. Information regarding her social situation prior to admission is required; this can be discussed with Mrs Hall and, bearing in mind her intermittent confusion, confirmation of the details is required from her next of kin, carers or friends. Assessment of personal care ability is carried out on the ward. Mrs Hall is also taken to the Occupational Therapy Department to be assessed further on her general mobility, her ability to get on and off furniture and in the kitchen. The occupational therapist assesses the level of confusion and understanding as well as physical ability. Standardised scored tests can be used by the occupational therapist as well as subjective observation. A home visit is used for further assessment in the home environment.

These problems and solutions were identified by the occupational therapist:

- Mrs Hall required prompting with personal care morning and evening and assistance with changing pads.
- Mrs Hall was unsafe in the use of hot kitchen equipment.
- Due to her fluctuating confusion Mrs Hall was unreliable re taking her medication.
- Bathing equipment was required along with physical help in its use.
- Two walking frames were needed at home – one for upstairs and one for downstairs.
- Continence was still an issue and Mrs Hall still struggled getting to the toilet, so two commodes (one for upstairs, one for downstairs) were ordered.
- A second stair rail will be installed.
- Key Safe installation will take place to allow carer access.
- Liaison is required with a District Nurse to ensure the provision of a pressure mattress and cushion, a continence assessment and monitoring of blood sugars.

- Liaison will also take place with a social worker to provide a care package to cover personal care, preparation of food/drinks, supervision and encouragement eating/drinking, emptying the commode and monitoring medication.
- A pendant alarm will be provided to call for help in case of a fall.

So as you can see, there is a lot to consider and the occupational therapy role is vital.'

The therapist in this case study ensured that the client was at the centre of the decision-making process regarding her return home. There were others who were involved in this process: the hospital team of nurses and medical staff will each have completed their own tasks in order that the occupational therapist can fulfil the final assessment. Each member of the multidisciplinary team will have their own responsibilities and they work effectively together. The family or carers of the client may also be included in the decision-making process. They will be involved in the long-term support of the patient and their circumstances should also be considered. This client-centred practice is one of those essential philosophies of the profession.

The next case study shows how an occupational therapist can be involved at the end of a person's life.

Case study: Working in Neuro-Oncology Occupational Therapy – Caroline Barber Miller

'A day in the life of an occupational therapist within Neuro-Oncology is never typical. The client group is highly unpredictable in nature with many variables and complexities which can create challenges. My routine commences at 8.00am with a review of emails and administration tasks. At 8.30am I join with colleagues for a daily handover of patients who are either in-patients or are at home and need urgent review by the occupational therapist.

In-patients requiring screening pre-discharge are prioritised and screened for functional and cognitive deficits. The patient's family will be included in conversations regarding discharge and I use clinical reasoning to determine the required interventions to facilitate a safe discharge. Any functional needs that are identified are met with further rehabilitation at a neuro-rehabilitation unit or a step-down facility. If I assess that my patient is safe for discharge then

I may need to order equipment to facilitate their independence at home. Sometimes this equipment can be delivered for me and other times I need to collect and deliver it myself, so that I can be assured that it is fitted safely and that I can train carers to use it. I always arrange to make either a follow-up telephone call or a review visit myself or arrange for a community rehabilitation team to follow up on any continuing needs. I ensure that I pass on all of this important information to the ward staff and the Neuro-Oncology team, so that no misunderstandings occur that could compromise the patient.

Next I make urgent visits to community patients to try to prevent unnecessary admission to hospital. Sometimes a problem may arise that I can resolve, enabling the person to remain at home. Typically these visits present with a patient who may or may not have insight into their difficulties, a very concerned and sometimes frightened and exhausted partner or carer who has struggled to carry on until the situation reaches crisis and they contact the nursing team. It is important to listen carefully to the carer as well as the patient, giving both private time to express their concerns. Understanding both points of view helps me to formulate better solutions.

I often use undertaking a meaningful occupation as a conduit to these conversations. For example, making a cup of tea is an everyday task that can serve many purposes. I can assess functional and cognitive capability whilst chatting about the problems. Doing this can help to relax the situation allowing the patient, carer and myself to talk through the situation and make a joint plan of intervention. This may include the provision of equipment, changes to sleeping environments – bringing a bed downstairs for example, making a referral to a Hospice, care agency, Macmillan or Marie Curie teams for financial advice, wheelchair and adaptation requests, carers assessments, telephone calls to GPs, the Neuro-Oncology nurses or the Consultants. I need to keep up to date with all of the local support agencies as well as the statutory services available for my patients and ensure that I make timely and accurate referrals.

Balancing the desires of the patient with the health and safety of their carer can be difficult, requiring patience and ingenuity. I need to use a range of interpersonal skills, especially when the information I have to give may not be what someone wants to hear. There are lots of ethical decisions that I have to make, always considering the best interests of my patient.

After carrying out my home visits I return to the office to complete electronic equipment and wheelchair orders, adaptations and hospice referrals. I make telephone calls to community services, palliative care, dietician and speech and language or rehabilitation teams to maximise the residual strength of patients. I follow up on the ongoing cases to ensure all my recommendations have been followed and respond to any new urgent issues. Time is unfortunately not on the side of my patients, so my ability to prioritise and problem-solve using evidence based practice without getting stressed myself is vitally important. This is when working as part of a supportive team is invaluable.'

Many prospective OT students say that they would like to work with children once they qualify. Here is an example of a day in the life of an occupational therapist working in paediatrics and the diversity of the role.

Case study: Working in children's occupational therapy – Kath Seddon

'One thing is certain – there are no two days in the life of a paediatric occupational therapist that are the same, or that are often very predictable for that matter – but that is one of the reasons that I enjoy the job so much.

Working with children, young people and their families is an enormous privilege. Being invited into a young person's home, their school and their family life to help them become more independent in achieving their everyday activities is anything but routine and quite frequently it presents enormous challenges, and I hope I can give you a little flavour of how we work.

In our community based service, we provide assessment and treatment to children between 0 and 19 years old. We cover the health and social care aspects of occupational therapy provision, which means that we can be involved in anything from making tiny splints for a newborn baby, to advising on a specialist housing adaptation for a young person with profound disabilities. On the same day we may run an assessment clinic or attend a care planning meeting with colleagues from a variety of different agencies. We may run a life skills group for children to develop their independence skills or present a training session for school teachers about topics such as fine motor skills or the sensory strategies they can use with children in their classrooms.

Today has been a pretty typical day which began with a school-based assessment for a young girl with Down's Syndrome. She was struggling to sit properly in class so that she could take part in her lessons and the teacher asked if I could give some advice. I quickly observed that she did not have enough postural support in her school chair. The desk was too high and she would continually stand, kneel and squirm in her chair as she tried to find a comfortable and stable position. Following my assessment, I have found a specialist classroom chair that gives her a much more supportive seating position. The results were amazing as she was able to sit more securely and focus on her work, producing some fantastic writing and drawing for me as well.

My next visit – another school based session, but this time to a young boy with autism and lots of difficulties with sensory issues. I worked with his teaching assistant on developing ideas to encourage him to participate in sensory play, such as using feely bags and exploring different textures and sensory experiences. I also came up with some ideas for sensory breaks during the day, to give him time to calm and regulate himself so that he could go back to focus on his schoolwork for a little longer. This approach is working well and his teaching assistant is really beginning to understand his behaviours from a sensory perspective now, which is great.

This afternoon has been filled with new appointments. One teenager who is struggling with handwriting coming up to her GCSEs because of hypermobility syndrome; a ten-year-old boy who is finding difficulty with motor skills tasks such as fastening shoe-laces, using a knife and fork and learning to ride a bike and finally a toddler who has been diagnosed with cerebral palsy and needs some help to use her right hand more successfully in her daily activities.

I certainly enjoy my varied role and look forward to all the different challenges it brings each day.'

This next occupational therapist shows how it is possible to balance a management role with a clinical role. Sharing expertise whilst still enjoying the face to face contact with clients can be a very rewarding role.

Case study: Working in learning disability occupational therapy – Caroline McGloin

'As a band 7 Occupational Therapy Clinical Lead in a learning disability service my days are a mixture of staffing and service issues, planning and clinical work. I am also providing cover for another clinical team which means juggling a few extra jobs too. My day starts with a quick occupational therapy staff meeting, a chance to check everyone is ok and all referrals have been allocated, to share information and discuss any concerns. After this I get a chance to quickly check my emails and return any calls before heading out on a busy clinic day.

Today I am working with my occupational therapy assistant to complete seven appointments for postural care needs; seating and sleep systems, with an external company representative. We get a large quantity of referrals and book appointments for the children and adults to our regular roaming clinics. We try to see people in the most appropriate setting, which may be their own homes, school, day services or respite. Sometimes we run clinics and people come to us for the assessment; however, seeing people at home allows us to also assess the home surroundings and we try to complete a review of other equipment in use at home, to ensure our records are up to date, at the same time.

The last appointment finishes at 5.30pm. We have seen seven clients as planned, completed four assessments, set up three pieces of specialist equipment, completed equipment checks for each person and identified three further pieces of work that need to be actioned. We also identified one issue that will need discussing with the safe guarding team for further advice.

Throughout the day as we travel between appointments my occupational therapy assistant and I discuss what happened on the visit to ensure the correct information has been recorded and we agree what the action plan is. My occupational therapy assistant will complete the clinical records and process any orders when she gets into the office tomorrow as I am out again all day at the directorate speciality Quality and Assurance Group and then at a meeting looking at how we implement the Purposeful and Productive Community Services agenda in our service. My day tomorrow will end checking and counter signing the clinical notes from today and completing any clinical justifications required for equipment provision, which the occupational therapy assistant is unable to do.

My days may be long but they are certainly varied!'

Many occupational therapists work in the community, helping people to remain at home and independent. The next occupational therapist uses her ability to analyse and prioritise in order to manage a large and unpredictable workload successfully.

Case study: Working in a Community Therapy – Katie Hatch

'I work as an occupational therapist within a Community Therapy Team. The Team consists of Occupational Therapists, Physiotherapists and Specialised Therapy Assistants. The aim of the Service is to try and maintain a person's independence and safety within their own home and prevent the need for hospital admission and the need for long-term care. Referrals are received from many different sources such as GPs, Social Workers, Community Nursing Teams, the patient or their family. The caseload consists of adults over the age of 18 and with a wide variety of medical conditions.

My day starts with triaging new referrals. This involves prioritising each referral and deciding when each new patient needs to be assessed and by which member of the team. Today an urgent referral was received from a GP requesting assessment of Jack who has had sudden onset of knee pain due to osteoarthritis and is having difficulty walking and carrying out activities of daily living such as meal preparation. I visited Jack at home and carried out a full assessment. This included finding out what his normal level of function was and gaining his perception of what he was having difficulty in undertaking at present. I then assessed the strength and range of movement in his upper and lower limbs, his balance and cognition and ability to carry out all his activities of daily living. I assessed his ability to walk and transfer on and off his furniture. I related this information to each of the activities that he had to undertake throughout the day. Jack had increased pain and reduced stability when walking therefore I provided him with a walking stick to provide additional support when walking. Jack was able to access his kitchen and maintain balance when reaching up and bending down into the cupboards and fridge; he demonstrated that he was able to use all appliances and utensils but had reduced standing tolerance and reduced ability to safely transport items from his kitchen to living room. I therefore provided him with a perching stool which he can sit on when preparing meals and he could also sit on this stool in the kitchen when eating his meals; by doing this it was decided that the need for home carers was not required. During the visit I also assessed Jack and his home environment for safety and risk of falls. It was identified that Jack became dizzy at times when standing up and when turning his head; there appeared to be a medical reason for this therefore I made a referral so that this could be investigated further.

My next visit was to Doris who has been receiving rehabilitation from the therapy team following a fractured hip and its surgical repair. Doris has been undertaking lower limb and balance exercises and mobility practice. Her mobility has increased and she is now able to access more rooms within her home. It was identified that she is currently feeling isolated from other family members as she has been unable to sit in a chair in the main living room in the evening due to it being low. She has been sitting in a riser recliner chair within her kitchen dining room, which is where she wants to remain throughout the day. Although this chair meets her physical needs, her mood is greatly affected as she is missing the social interaction and watching television each evening with the rest of her family. I therefore raised the chair in the living room with furniture raisers and observed that independent transfers could now be carried out. Due to having hip surgery Doris was unable to bend to be able to wash and dress her lower body. I provided her with a long handled sponge and shoe horn, a sock aid and a "helping hand" to assist her in undertaking these tasks. This was really beneficial to Doris who felt that she would be less dependent on her family and carers. Although this has been a relatively non-complex case I found it to be rewarding as I know that I had made a real difference to Doris, not only to her physically but also emotionally.

The rest of the day consisted of liaising with other health and social care professionals regarding patients on my caseload, making referrals to the equipment store and adaptations team and writing notes. No one day is the same as my caseload is so varied. I plan my visits for the next day, knowing that this could change depending on the urgent referrals that are received. One thing that is for certain is that the next day will be challenging but also interesting and worthwhile.'

Our next example is in another specialised service. Here group work and one to one interventions are designed by the occupational therapist, to enable service users to achieve their goals.

Case study: Working in an Eating Disorders Day Service – Rebecca Noon

'I work as a Specialist Occupational Therapist within an Intensive Eating Disorders Day Service for adults. The service supports service users, predominantly with Anorexia Nervosa, to avoid hospital admission, transition from hospital to the community, treat relapse and offers an alternative to a hospital setting. Service users can attend from 8am–6pm Monday to Friday and will spend evenings and weekends at home. Service users will be assessed to attend the Day Service in terms of motivation and physical risks. The team consists of a Doctor, Nursing Staff, Dietitians, Psychologist, Art Therapist, support staff and of course Occupational Therapists.

My typical day usually involves facilitating a breakfast, lunch or evening meal preparation and eating group. Each service user participating will have undergone a Model of Human Occupation Screening Tool (MOHOST) observational assessment and Eating and Meal Preparation Assessment (EMPSA). This enables the group to be graded appropriately to suit the needs of each service user. My recommendations are made to support service users with functional preparation skills, reducing eating disordered behaviours and improving their coping strategies. Another group I facilitate is a recovery group which involves service users working through a recovery workbook. I help service users to think about their triggers, stress vulnerability, coping strategies, use of time and SMART goal setting. I also facilitate a social eating group. This again involves outcomes of the EMPSA and MOHO assessment tools to assess and grade the group accordingly. The group follows a structured intervention plan working on individual and group goals to eat out in a variety of environments and social settings. A frequent goal of service users is to be able to eat out again in university/college canteens or to be able to join in with friends and family celebratory meals out. Skills to improve money management, exploring meaningful activities, using public transport, assertiveness and improving social skills are also topics that service users identify as important to them.

I undertake 1:1 assessments using a wide variety of assessment tools. Following this the interventions follow specific individualised goal setting. An example of this would be working with a service user to return to university. This involves working on coping strategies, recovery planning and a graded return to university in conjunction with treatment. Other 1:1 intervention may involve working towards goals around being able to eat with family. I create a graded plan with the service user to start eating with staff, other service users, participate in meal groups and then transfer these skills to the home environment. Service users often want to work on their eating disordered behaviours including portioning skills, challenging feared foods, normalising maladaptive behaviours and managing distress when eating. I use my skills of grading, adapting and problem-solving to ensure the therapeutic activities and motivational goals I suggest enable service users to work on these needs.

My role is very rewarding and enables me to use my core occupational therapy skills. It is a vital role in supporting service users in their recovery from an eating disorder.'

Many more graduates are considering taking a role in an emerging area of practice. Here is an example of transferring occupational therapy skills effectively and getting huge job satisfaction.

Case study: Working in the charity sector – Fiona Baker

'When I was at university listening to lectures about role emerging occupational therapy jobs, I couldn't see myself in anything other than the NHS. Now, two role emerging jobs down the line, I can't see myself in anything other than a role emerging job, or more specifically, a charity sector job. I secured my graduate job with Age UK North Yorkshire and fell in love with the charity. I took a break to go gallivanting around the world and when I returned the opportunity arose for a job with Age UK Teesside and I jumped at it. My ID badge might say "Dementia Services Coordinator" and not "Occupational Therapist" but the work I do is occupational therapy through and through.

Charity sector work often involves project work, so the first few months are spent laying the foundations and wondering just how you're going to get any referrals into your service! Then one day it just clicks, suddenly your name and project is out there and referrals are coming at you thick and fast. Referrals can come from all areas including health, social care, other charities, work colleagues running other projects, or even self referrals walking in the front door.

Once the referrals have been received I visit the service users in their home and complete an initial assessment and DEMQOL assessment (a dementia specific assessment used to assess quality of life), which will be used as my outcome measure for the service user and for when the funding bids are due. Using my occupational therapy training in assessment I am able to ascertain whether group work or one to one therapy is more appropriate, and provide referrals into other services if necessary.

The therapy I'm currently providing is Maintenance Cognitive Stimulation Therapy, an evidence based treatment recommended by NICE for people with mild to moderate dementia. Sessions aim to actively engage and stimulate people with dementia, and service users usually always leave laughing! The flexibility I have whilst working in the charity sector really allows me to get to know the individuals, build up strong therapeutic relationships and tailor my therapy exactly to their needs. Although recording facts and figures is important, comments like "I felt poorly today, but you've made me feel better", "I had a lovely time with happy, friendly people", "Mum completed a word search today for the first time in years" and "I can't go out so I look forward to having your company each week" are the important parts of data gathering in my day to day practice.

Charity sector work might not pay quite as well as the statutory sector, but in my eyes, happiness comes before money. I genuinely look forward to work, as I'm surrounded by some of the most kind hearted colleagues and volunteers, who are completely passionate about their line of work. We are able to pick up where the NHS has had to finish, so can reach some of the most in need clients and provide that extra lifeline.

Occupational therapy is no longer just about sticking to the standard jobs, it's about flying the occupational therapy flag and looking at how our unique and transferable skills can benefit a whole range of services.'

Finally, here is a typical Monday for a student occupational therapist during an academic teaching block. Taking responsibility for your own learning and being motivated to make the most of the opportunities and facilities for learning should help you to succeed.

Case study: Studying Occupational Therapy – Jayde Kirkup

'I always knew I wanted to study Occupational Therapy from a young age, as I was born with cerebral palsy. Hospitals, operations and home adaptions were a big part of my life, as well as missing a lot of school. I am so glad that I am at Teesside University studying about such a unique and brilliant profession that enables people to overcome boundaries to regain independence.

I currently live with my Mum and my four siblings; I am the oldest of five. People usually think a full-time course is from Monday to Friday, when in fact it is Monday to Sunday if you include the work you do in your own time to prepare. On a usual Monday morning before starting university, I wake up at 8am to get ready for the day. I like to be organised and motivated, so on my bedroom wall I have a calendar that I made and each month is set out individually. On the calendars I have circled each date that has an assignment due or any other important dates so that it's easier to keep on top of deadlines. Days, weeks and months tend to blur into one. Therefore, by having each calendar month visually on my wall where I can cross off a day each morning, it motivates me to make the most out of the day by seeing that next assignment around the corner!

I drive to university and it can take anything from 30 minutes to over an hour depending on the traffic. My first morning lecture usually begins at 10am and this helps me to manage my fatigue levels as I miss the majority of the morning traffic. This particular lecture lasts for two hours and covers topics around evidence-based practice and how to critically appraise a research paper to improve future occupational therapy practice. Before the lecture begins, I make sure I have my laptop with the lecture PowerPoint slides on it. This makes it much easier and faster to document notes as my hand and arm can become physically tired and painful when writing for a period of time.

After this lecture I have a dinner break for one hour; I usually eat in the library and plan for the next lectures ahead. My afternoon consists of two separate lectures that last three hours in total. They cover a wide range of topics about clinical conditions, understanding client narratives and the assessment and evaluation tools that can be used in the occupational therapy process.

A full university day usually ends at 4pm, so I make the most of my time by going to the library to do some independent study. I actually like this part of the day as I get more work done there than I do at home. In the library, I tend to find a spot in the quiet zone where I can concentrate on planning or completing assignments. I can genuinely sit there working, with a hazelnut soya latte from Costa, for three hours. I do a lot of reading and typing during this time but it really is important to make that time for self-directed study. I usually drive back home after that to relax for a new day to start again.'

Chapter summary

The life of an occupational therapist is very varied and, as can be seen from these examples and those throughout this book, there is no one typical day. The demands of practice will require a therapist to draw on the full range of personal attributes to be successful in their work. The common theme throughout these stories is that the service user is at the centre of treatment. Becoming an occupational therapist is an enriching experience which will change lives: not only those you work with but also your own.

Key points

- Take the time to speak to occupational therapists and find out what they do each day.
- If possible look for opportunities to shadow an occupational therapist in order that you can understand more fully the nature of the relationship they have with their clients.
- Try to explore a variety of occupational therapy settings in order that you gain some insight into the breadth of work occupational therapists might be involved in.

Useful resources

NHS Health Careers: www.healthcareers.nhs.uk/explore-roles/allied-health-professionals/occupational-therapist

Step into the NHS: www.stepintothenhs.nhs.uk/careers/occupational-therapist

National Careers Service: https://nationalcareersservice.direct.gov.uk

The College of Occupational Therapists: www.cot.co.uk/become-ot

Index

BPP UNIVERSITY SCHOOL OF HEALTH

N

O

P

R

S

T

U

W